PLAYS BY
LOUIS PHILLIPS

D0840093

56 E 81st St., NY NY 10028–0202
212–772–8334/FAX 772–8358

PLAYS BY LOUIS PHILLIPS
© Copyright 1995 by Louis Phillips

First printing: December 1995
ISBN: 0-88145-118-5

Book design: Marie Donovan
Word processing: Microsoft Word for Windows 2.0a
Typographic controls: Xerox Ventura Publisher 2.0 PE
Typeface: Palatino
Printed on recycled acid-free paper and bound in the USA.

CONTENTS

ABOUT THE AUTHOR

Louis Phillips is a widely published poet, playwright, and short-story author. His published full-length plays include: THE ENVOI MESSAGES (Broadway Play Publishing Inc), THE BALLROOM IN ST PATRICK'S CATHEDRAL, and SIXTEEN POINTS ON A HURRICANE'S COMPASS (Aran Press), plus FRANKENSTEIN VIRTUOSO and KOPS (Prologue Press).

His full-length plays have been performed in New York City and in regional theaters. The Colonnades Theater Lab, under the direction of Michael Lessac, produced WARBECK and THE BALLROOM IN ST PATRICK'S CATHEDRAL. Indiana Rep produced THE ENVOI MESSAGES, directed by Ed Stern; and the Old Globe Theater in San Diego produced THE LAST OF THE MARX BROTHERS' WRITERS, directed by Craig Noel and starring Victor Bono. Alan Schneider directed Mr Phillips' play THE GREAT AMERICAN QUIZ SHOW SCANDAL at the University of California at San Diego.

In addition, Mr Phillips has written over thirty one-act plays. His one-acts have been published in *The Georgia Review, Massachusetts Review, Nassau Review, Aethlon,* and many other literary magazines. His one-act play GOIN' WEST was included in THE BEST SHORT PLAYS '87. THE MAN WHO ATE EINSTEIN'S BRAIN, produced by Roger Simon, has been performed in N Y C and broadcast on radio.

He currently lives in Manhattan with his wife Pat Ranard and their ten-year-old twin sons Ian and Matthew.

For
Robert Milgrom
&
Doris Maat
May your marriage have a longer run
than these short plays

ACKNOWLEDGMENTS

The author gratefully acknowledges the following people who have contributed so much in making this slender collection possible: Tom Eagan of Aran Press, who so graciously released the publishing rights to THE MAN WHO ATE EINSTEIN'S BRAIN; Roger Hendricks Simon who put so much time and energy into producing the aforesaid play; Jan Ross, who produced and directed CARWASH and BONE THE SPEED near Princeton and beyond; Marsh Cassidy who first published CARWASH in *CrazyQuilt*, and then included it in his anthology of modern one-acts; and last, but not least, Kip Gould who, through all these years, has kept the faith and his word.

BONE THE SPEED

CHARACTERS

Ross Hilary Hurok
Cardinal Menzel Cordobas
Michelle LaDon

(We are in the inner sanctum of ROSS HILARY HUROK, *chief executive officer and founder of Galaxy Motion Picture Co, a company that does not have nearly as many stars as there are in heaven, but has enough economic and artistic clout to rank with the top five film producers in the world. To list all the films released by Galaxy would take a book—a thin book—but a book nonetheless, and since we do not have a book at our disposal, we shall merrily take in a few of the posters [some bright, some lurid, some designed in the styles of David Hockney and Andy Warhol and Grandma Moses]: ROLLERHEAD ON MARS, ROLLERHEAD IV, RACING WITH THE SUN, MIAMI MON AMOUR, and A BRIEF HISTORY OF TIME.)*

(As the lights come up, HUROK *is on the phone. He is on the phone more often than not. His art is the art of the deal and, if you insist [as I would not] on knowing what he looks like and what he is like, you may read full-length plays by David Mamet, Arthur Kopit, Kaufman and Hart, Elmer Rice, Rod Serling, and twenty to thirty other playwrights who have been in the belly of the beast and have come back with tales to sicken your soul. Suffice to say this* HUROK *is no different than the others; nor is this play, for that matter. After all, a genre is a genre.)*

HUROK

(On the phone) That's right, Andre, I want Hockney's "A Visit with Christopher and Don, Santa Monica Canyon, 1984." I just saw a reproduction of it in *Variety* and you've got to get it for me.... I don't care what it costs. Get it for me! *(Down goes the receiver. He presses one of his intercom's buttons.)* O K, Josie, send Joey Bishop in.

(The great doors open and CARDINAL MENZEL CORDOBAS *enters.* CARDINAL CORDOBAS, *fully robed, is a splendid looking, sun-tanned man in his early fifties.)*

HUROK

(Rising, crossing) Hey, Joey, baby... *(Pauses)* Wait a minute! You're not Joey Bishop.... What happened to Joey Bishop for chrissakes?

CARDINAL CORDOBAS

(With appropriate dignity) I am Cardinal Cordobas of the Beverly Hills Diocese. I believe your secretary scheduled this appointment several months ago.

HUROK

Holy Mary Mother of God! A real cardinal! And I thought I had an appointment with a comedian.... Forgive me, your Most Holy Excellency, you've caught me off-guard.... My secretary wrote down 'Bishop' and I just assumed....

CARDINAL CORDOBAS

It happens to me all the time....

HUROK

I bet it does.... Sit here, Your Excellency...in the light... Can I get you something to drink? *(He opens his considerable liquor cabinet.)*

CARDINAL CORDOBAS

Some port if you have it....

HUROK

Port? A little Smith Woodhouse 1976 late bottled vintage Porto.... Wait a minute. *(Visibly stiffens)* You're not one of my goddamned extras all dressed up, trying to pull a stunt on me, are you?

CARDINAL CORDOBAS

I assure you, Mr Hurok, I am an authentic cardinal, formerly a bishop, appointed by the Vatican.

HUROK

The Vatican, eh?

CARDINAL CORDOBAS

Pope Paul himself...but *in petto*, of course.

HUROK

In petto?

CARDINAL CORDOBAS

Literally 'in the breast'. It's a term applied to cardinals appointed by the Pope but not named in the Consistory. You see, the Pope felt it was not a good idea for word to get out that a cardinal had been assigned to Beverly Hills.

CENTER HUROK

Well, he's wrong about that. Nothing improves religious fervor like a little action on Rodeo Drive.

CARDINAL CORDOBAS

Yes. That's one reason I'm here.

HUROK

Well, it would have to be important if you're a real cardinal because I have fallen away from Catholicism years ago.... Or, it fell way from me. *(Attends to the port)* On ice?

CARDINAL CORDOBAS

Straight up.

HUROK

I've never entertained a cardinal before.... Every so often a few priests drop in to request a special showing of *Going My Way*...or to ask me to talk on Joan of Arc. I am somewhat of an authority on Joan of Arc....

CARDINAL CORDOBAS

I've never visited a motion picture studio before....

HUROK

You must let me give you a tour.... Maybe you have a favorite movie star you would like to meet.

CARDINAL CORDOBAS

Marie Dressler....

HUROK

Marie Dressler? My God, she must be dead for about fifty years.

CARDINAL CORDOBAS

I know.

HUROK

I suppose we could have her dug up for you, but wouldn't you
prefer something more up to date, something a little more lively?
Sexy?... In pure confidence, Your Excellency, Marie Dressler looked
like hell in a bikini.

CARDINAL CORDOBAS

I was merely joking, Mr Hurok....

HUROK

Call me Ross...

CARDINAL CORDOBAS

You see, Mr Hurok...Ross...even cardinals have their quirks.

HUROK

I bet they do.... But I wasn't kidding about the tour. I'll have my
secretaries fix you up with a free pass. We have a whole special
effects building for the tourists. They think the Empire State Building
is falling on them. You should hear the screams of terror. I bet the
church could pick up four or five conversions a pop.... I've taken the
tour of St Patrick's Cathedral in Manhattan and what's that all about?
A few windows you can't see through and a wax statue of a pope
under glass. That's not going to get anybody excited. The Catholic
Church should have something like we have.

CARDINAL CORDOBAS

It's certainly something to think about.

HUROK

The Resurrection was the last special effects your religion has had....
(Holds up his glass) Do you have a special toast?

CARDINAL CORDOBAS

(Smiles) Anything in Latin.

HUROK

(Joining the jest) Anything in Latin, huh? You think that's got me
stumped?

CARDINAL CORDOBAS

Cheers!

HUROK

Forget cheers... Try this one, Your Excellency: In flagrante delicto...

CARDINAL CORDOBAS

In flagrante delicto...

HUROK

Outside of ars por gratis ars it's the only Latin I know.

CARDINAL CORDOBAS

Ah, well, I asked for it.

HUROK

Yes, you did.... Wait. I thought of a third. Si non oscillas, noli tintinnare.

CARDINAL CORDOBAS

Si non oscillas, noli tintinnare?

HUROK

If you don't swing, don't ring.That bit of Latin is actually carved over Hugh Hefner's bedroom door.

CARDINAL CORDOBAS

I'm not familiar with it.

HUROK

Well, two of three's bad.... Now, what can I do for you, Your Excellency? I hope this is not official.

CARDINAL CORDOBAS

What do you mean by official?

HUROK

Like maybe you know something I don't. My doctor probably called you to tell you I am drawing my final breath right now and you've rushed over in your Mercedes to pronounce Extreme Unction.

CARDINAL CORDOBAS

Not exactly. And I don't own a Mercedes.

HUROK

(Pours more wine) What exactly?

CARDINAL CORDOBAS
A customized Dusenberg.

HUROK
I meant what exactly did you come for?

CARDINAL CORDOBAS
I've come to inquire about one of your stars....

HUROK
Which one?

CARDINAL CORDOBAS
Michelle LaDon.

HUROK
Michelle LaDon? What's that bitch up to now?

CARDINAL CORDOBAS
We hope nothing but good works because we want to make her a saint.

HUROK
(Spits out his wine) A saint? You want to make Michelle LaDon a saint?

CARDINAL CORDOBAS
I have official instructions from the pope.... The Catholic Church needs a new saint. We want it to be her.

HUROK
Your Excellency, if we could be serious.... I am on a tight schedule. In a few minutes Michelle LaDon is going to be here to rehearse the theme song to *Fort Lauderdale, Mon Amour*. I know cardinals have their quirks, but making fun of movie producers should not be one of them. You never know when a man like me could prove useful to the church.

CARDINAL CORDOBAS
Mr Hurok...Ross...that's exactly why I am here. To see how useful you can be. I am serious. For decades now, the Catholic Church has been losing worshippers by the millions. The time has come to take

the bull—even it's only a papal bull—by the horns. We need new images to make the young people sit up and take notice.

CENTER HUROK

But Michelle LaDon is no saint!

CARDINAL CORDOBAS

Of course not. Nobody's a saint until the Church makes them one. There are a few formalities to be observed, but in Ms LaDon's case I am certain there should be no problems. The pope has expressed willingness to gloss over a few things....

HUROK

A few things? Michelle LaDon has slept with every man on the lot, some thirty or forty of the women, and four tour guides. I've even seen her hanging around with members of the union. How low can a person fall?

CARDINAL CORDOBAS

A little exuberant sexuality need not detain the soul from entering into a state of grace.

HUROK

Exuberant sexuality isn't the phrase I would use. Try nymphomania.... Oh, why should I be polite? She's a whore.

CARDINAL CORDOBAS

Are you not familiar with the story of Christ and Mary Magdalene?

HUROK

I gave it a courtesy read once.

CARDINAL CORDOBAS

I don't mean to upset you.

HUROK

You haven't upset me.

CARDINAL CORDOBAS

I've upset you.

HUROK
(Visibly upset) You haven't upset me! I am merely mystified why, out of all the persons you could choose for sainthood, you have fastened upon Michelle LaDon. What's wrong Annette Funicello? Or Mother Teresa?

CARDINAL CORDOBAS
(Rising from his chair) Mother Teresa isn't popular enough. You see, for decades now it has become obvious to the leaders of the Church that there is only one religion in America, one religion in the world perhaps, and that religion is not, alas, Catholicism. Nor Buddhism. Nor Hinduism. Judaism. No, the one religion in the world is movies. The young worship movie stars, not Christ. Children grow up with the images of Mickey Mouse and Donald Duck, not the image of Christ suffering on the cross. Why, when James Dean died, his fans ripped out portions of their skin and offered themselves up as human sacrifice. No one did that when Christ died.

HUROK
Then make James Dean a saint and leave Michelle LaDon alone!

CARDINAL CORDOBAS
We shall. James Dean is on the list, right after E T and Doris Day. E T because he has taught us how to love creatures unlike ourselves, and Doris Day because she has taught us to remain virgins while doing so. But first we need someone more up-to-date, someone who speaks to the young women of today.

HUROK
Why not the young men?

CARDINAL CORDOBAS
Because if we can get women back into the church, the men are sure to follow.

HUROK
You mean the great cathedrals of Europe are going to be changed into singles bars?

CARDINAL CORDOBAS
No. What I am trying to tell you is that the Vatican is going to do everything in its considerable power to bring men, women,

children—and that most despicable of all of God's creations, teen-agers—back into the fold.... Even you have to admit, in spite of all the terrible things you have said about her, that Michelle LaDon is the most popular singer, dancer, actress in the world today.

HUROK

Don't get me wrong, Your Eminence. I'm fond of the woman. Truly fond of her. In petto, of course.

CARDINAL CORDOBAS

In petto?

HUROK

In the breasts.

CARDINAL CORDOBAS

In the breast.

HUROK

To each his own.

CARDINAL CORDOBAS

I imaging that when it comes to breasts it can be no other way.... Why, Ms LaDon's breasts and every other part of her make headlines. Since everyone worships her already, why not worship her within the confines and dogma of an already established religion? If Coca Cola can use Michael Jackson to sell its product, why can't religion do likewise? And we have a more profound message.

HUROK

Why are you telling me all this? Michelle LaDon is the one you should be talking to.

CARDINAL CORDOBAS

Well, we have talked to her agent. Ms LaDon is very difficult to speak to in person. Still, the agent seems amenable. Many actresses receive Oscars; few, if any, ever become saints.

HUROK

(Sighs) Tell me about it.

CARDINAL CORDOBAS
But you have her under contract for four more films. The pope
would like you to release her from her contract.

HUROK
Release Michelle LaDon from her contract?

CARDINAL CORDOBAS
The Vatican will provide appropriate remuneration, of course.

HUROK
For someone of Ms LaDon's stature there is no appropriate
remuneration.

CARDINAL CORDOBAS
$30,000,000?

HUROK
$30,000,000? Michelle LaDon will gross $300,000,000 worldwide.

CARDINAL CORDOBAS
Gross. Let's talk net.

HUROK
For a cardinal you don't leave your business sense outside.

CARDINAL CORDOBAS
If I left my business sense outside, I would never have become
cardinal.

HUROK
Then don't offer me peanuts for diamonds.

CARDINAL CORDOBAS
We're prepared to offer you $750,000,000 to take over Ms LaDon's
contract and to buy your studio.

HUROK
Buy my studio?

CARDINAL CORDOBAS
I'm telling you the Vatican is serious about reaching out to the
world's peoples in a new way.

(One of the many buzzers on HUROK's *desk sounds.* HUROK *responds immediately.)*

HUROK

Yes, Josie?

VOICE OF JOSIE

Ms LeDon is here. Can you see her?

HUROK

Just give me five minutes.

VOICE OF JOSIE

Yes, Sir.

HUROK

(To CARDINAL CORDOBAS*)* The Vatican wants to make movies?
The public can take the life of Christ every fifty years or so.
Religious movies mean death at the box office. They're worse than
movies about writers and/or fly fishermen. Look at me. For years,
I've wanted to produce and direct a new version of Joan of Arc.
I can't get the backing. I even had the idea B P.

CARDINAL CORDOBAS

B P?

HUROK

Before Preminger.

CARDINAL CORDOBAS

We don't want to make religious movies. We want to make
movies religious. We want to take your standard product and
add subliminal messages.

HUROK

Subliminal messages?

CARDINAL CORDOBAS

Yes, you know. Written words on the screen flashed at such a high
rate of speed that the eye can't see them, but the brain still takes them
in.

HUROK

I know what they are. We use them to sell popcorn.

CARDINAL CORDOBAS

Well, let's use them to sell Christ. In the middle of your popular
Rollerhead series, we could insert messages such as LOVE THY
NEIGHBOR. Or GO TO CHURCH ON SUNDAY. THINK
CATHOLIC.

HUROK

Won't it be slightly contradictory? I mean, showing a scene of
futuristic warriors blowing up a planet while the words LOVE
THY NEIGHBOR flash?

CARDINAL CORDOBAS

Human beings are contradictory by nature. That's why they need
a strong religion to present them a noncontradictory view of life.
Human lives meander all over the place. Religion puts a premium
on the straight and narrow.

HUROK

Don't do it.

CARDINAL CORDOBAS

Don't do what?

HUROK

Take my advice. The less your church has to do with innovation the
better. First, you tried Bingo games. And what did Bingo do? You
merely had old ladies living from Wednesday night to Wednesday
night instead of Sunday to Sunday. Next, you—though I'm not
talking about you personally, Your Holy Eminence, but those who
control dogma, creed, and ritual—decided that no one understood
Latin and so now Masses are spoken in English. What sounded so
beautiful and mystical in Latin sounded like a shopping list in
English. You forgot that people don't attend church to understand.
Understanding we get at the local bar and grill. We go to church to
be awed by that which we don't understand. Finally, to lure the
faithless back, a decision was handed down to replace the Gregorian
chant with progressive jazz.

CARDINAL CORDOBAS

When I first entered you recommended special effects. A tour
through the Resurrection complete with simulated earthquakes.

HUROK

I was kidding...kidding!

CARDINAL CORDOBAS

The pope is not. What is at stake are people's souls.... Perhaps you
will think better of our proposal if you also take into consideration
that the church is willing to loan you some artwork from its extensive
private collection.

HUROK

Does it have David Hockney's "A Visit With Christopher and Don,
Santa Monica Canyon 1984"?

CARDINAL CORDOBAS

If it were purchased by a Catholic perhaps there is a chance we can
get it for you.

(The intercom sounds again.)

VOICE OF JOSIE

Mr Hurok, Ms LaDon says if you keep her waiting for thirty more
seconds, she is taking her, and I quote, "Golden ass" through the
portals of Galaxy Films—never to return.

HUROK

What are you waiting for? Send her right in.... No, Your Holy
Eminence, the church must not cheapen its product by pandering
to the masses...or even to the Mass.

CARDINAL CORDOBAS

We are not cheapening anything. We are merely making Catholicism
more desirable. Besides, it's not only worshippers who are walking
away, the church is suffering a shortage of priests. In 1970, there were
at least 37,000 active diocesan priests serving 50,000,000 Catholics.
Today there are fewer than 25,000 priests. By the year 2000 we may
have only 18,000 priests. And even the clergy we do get are not
always the best qualified. Thus, desperate measures must be taken.

HUROK

Have you considered prayer?

CARDINAL CORDOBAS

Prayer is not desperate.

HUROK

Whoever said that has never produced a movie.

(On the word "movie" the doors to HUROK's *office fling open and who should appear but* MICHELLE LADON, *and if she is not everything you imagined her to be then this play has no further need to go on scaling the heights of Mount Parnassus.* MICHELLE *is blonde, slender, and dressed in a thin, see-through gown that leaves little to the imagination. She chews gum vigorously and wears a gold cross around her swanlike throat. If you wish to know more about her, feel free to read Mamet, Kopit, Rice, Bud Schulberg, et al. We humble mortals can only do so much.)*

HUROK

(Rising, if he has not already arisen) Michelle...do come in.... *(He throws himself on his knees and gathers the hem of her dress to his lips.)* Oh, Most Holy Saint of Cinema, may I kiss the hem of your virgin garments.

MICHELLE

Cut the crap, willya, Ross, or I'll have a stigmata placed upon your testicles.... Oh, I see Cardinal Cordobas has been filling you in on the details....

HUROK

(Rising, if he has not already arisen) You've met?

MICHELLE

No, but he and his backers have cut a deal with my agent. And Josie told me who you were meeting with.

HUROK

Whom I was meeting with.... Cardinal Cordobas, may I present you Michelle LaDon.

MICHELLE

(Curtsies) Charmed, I'm sure.

CARDINAL CORDOBAS

What an extreme pleasure to finally meet you in person, Ms LaDon.

MICHELLE

Call me Michelle... What do I call you?

HUROK

Try "Your Holy Eminence".

MICHELLE

Your Holy Eminence? That's a bit much, isn't it?

HUROK

Well, His Holy Eminence is a cardinal.

MICHELLE

Well, I'm going to be a saint for Chrissakes. What are people going to call me?

HUROK

I'm certain we'll think of something.

MICHELLE

I love you too, darling.

HUROK

Scotch and soda?

MICHELLE

Now that I am on the path to sainthood, I'm giving up drinking.

HUROK

Come on, Michelle, you don't really want want to be a saint?

MICHELLE

Of course I do. My agent says it will be good for my career.

HUROK

Career? Saints don't have careers. Saints don't even have agents. Imagine what havoc that would be. Suppose a cripple came to you to be healed. You can't say, call my agent first.

MICHELLE

I'm not going to cure cripples.

HUROK

Whom are you going to cure? The healthy? That will be novel.
Not to mention redundant.

MICHELLE

(Appeals to CARDINAL CORDOBAS *for help)* You see, Father, how he
treats me?

CARDINAL CORDOBAS

Ms LaDon is going to be our Patron Saint of Cinema, the first saint of
the movies.

MICHELLE

Images of me are going to be in every motion picture theater in the
country.

CARDINAL CORDOBAS

At the head of every video tape.

MICHELLE

Whenever and wherever a motion picture is shown, my name will be
spoken... *(To* HUROK*)* with reverence, you rat!

HUROK

I'm deeply moved. I truly am. I can't wait until I light a candle to you
in front of the buttered popcorn.

MICHELLE

Why are you so cynical?

HUROK

Because I live in L A and have to commute to work every morning.

CARDINAL CORDOBAS

Are you going to release Ms LaDon from her contract or not?

HUROK

Of course not.

MICHELLE

You bastard! Are you going to keep me from sainthood?

HUROK

No. You are.

MICHELLE

What's that suppose to mean?

HUROK

First of all, saints are supposed to be dead...long dead.... You need
to be burnt at the stake or something. Because if people were sainted
while still alive they might do something to fuck up their sainthood!
Forgive my French, Your Holiness.

MICHELLE

Is he right, Father?... Your Holiness...am I going to be put to death?
It sounds to me as if sainthood is no fun if you can't be around to
enjoy it.

CARDINAL CORDOBAS

Of course not my child. We explained it all to your agent. In your
case, the Vatican is willing to waive a few rules. Because your movies
and concerts have brought so much joy to hundreds of millions of
peoples, the pope is going to designate you as the First Living Saint,
the Saint of Cinema.

MICHELLE

(To HUROK) See? I told you so.

HUROK

And secondly, saints must experience suffering.

MICHELLE

Well, I'm not wearing any hairshirts.

HUROK

I'm not talking about hairshirts. I'm talking about great suffering.
The kind invoked by Bette Davis and Joan Crawford at their finest....
It is a saint's suffering that brings her mercy, compassion, and
wisdom. What does Ms LaDon know about suffering?

MICHELLE

I work for you, don't I?

HUROK

Her idea of suffering is to swim in an unheated pool.

CARDINAL CORDOBAS

Mr Hurok...

HUROK

Ross...

CARDINAL CORDOBAS

What makes you such an authority on sainthood?

HUROK

Because, as I told you earlier, I have spent a great deal of my leisure time studying Joan of Arc, and because the church and I are roughly in the same business. We create images for the public to worship. At the moment worshippers just happen to be flocking to my temple instead of to yours. Maybe that's why I don't wish to release Ms LaDon from her contract. I like being my own priest. One who has not taken a vow of poverty.

MICHELLE

When I'm a saint, I want him excommunicated. I want to see him burn in Hell forever and ever. There must be a Hell for movie producers.

HUROK

There is. It's called Losing Money at the Box Office.... And you, in spite of your human frailties, are still big B O.

MICHELLE

B O you S O B?

HUROK

Is this a spelling bee?... As far as I'm concerned, as soon as we wrap *Fort Lauderdale, Mon Amour*, you're still going to do four more pictures for me.

MICHELLE

(To CARDINAL CORDOBAS) He knows what he can do with his contract, because even if he doesn't release me, I'll take a hike. What's he going to do? Drag a saint into court? What judge in his right mind is going to find a saint guilty? If saints were guilty they wouldn't be saints.

CARDINAL CORDOBAS

Well, I think I'll let you two finish your business....

MICHELLE

He and I are finished.... Believe you me.

CARDINAL CORDOBAS

If you will allow me, I shall go home, call the Vatican, and see what our next move should be. I'm certain that, in the interest of world peace, we should be able to come to terms. We had hoped for your cooperation, but.... If not, ah well... The church has waited nearly 2,000 years to come to terms with mass media. I'm certain we can wait a little longer, and then, my son, I think there will be a good chance of your coming up empty-handed. A very good chance.... (He starts toward the door.)

HUROK

Wait! Your Holiness, I have been thinking of a proposition that might be of interest to the Vatican....

CARDINAL CORDOBAS

And what is that?

HUROK

Joan of Arc!

CARDINAL CORDOBAS

Joan of Arc?

MICHELLE

Joan of Arc? I don't even speak French.

HUROK

Imagine Michelle as France's beloved Joan! I've always wanted to do a film of Joan of Arc, now you've given me the perfect opportunity. If the Vatican will underwrite production costs, help with the publicity, require devout Catholics to see it, for example, then I'll let Michelle go after one more picture.

CARDINAL CORDOBAS
It is appropriate subject matter....

HUROK
It's a perfect stepstone for Michelle. From playing Joan of Arc she can become Joan of Arc. Tied to the stake of crass commercialism and hype, her soul ascends toward heaven.

MICHELLE
I don't want to play no saint. I want to be one. There's a difference.

HUROK
How can we tell. In Hollywood, reality and illusion are inextricably intertwined.... Look, Michelle, this will be the greatest coup in motion picture history. You'll get an Oscar and sainthood in the same year. No one will ever beat that combination.

MICHELLE
Don't listen to him, Father. He knows how to swing the malarky.

(HUROK *is dragging a coat rack to the center of the room.*)

HUROK
No, no. Look at this great moment. Michelle as Joan tied to the stake.... Come here, darling.... Show His Eminence the single greatest moment in cinema history....

(*He takes* MICHELLE *by the wrist and leads her to the coat rack. She strikes the appropriate pose.*)

HUROK
If that's not sainthood, then I don't know what is.... Look, let me make it look more authentic....

(*He removes his belt and ties* MICHELLE's *arms around the rack.*)

MICHELLE
What are you doing?

HUROK
Adding authenticity to the scene....

MICHELLE
Autheticity? With a Pierre Cardin belt? What kind of circles do you think Joan of Arc travelled in?

HUROK
There are things about saints the church never tells about....

(Our producer, after making certain that Joan of Arc is fastened to the stake, now empties his wastepaper basket at her feet.)

MICHELLE
Stop that! You're getting carbon paper over my stockings.

HUROK
Pretend these papers are faggots waiting to be lit...

CARDINAL CORDOBAS
I've seen Otto Preminger's version.... I think I get the idea.

HUROK
Preminger! I'm not talking Preminger! I'm talking B P.

CARDINAL CORDOBAS
B P?

HUROK
Beyond Preminger!

(He takes out his cigarette lighter, opens it, and pours lighter fluid onto the papers.)

HUROK
We'll just add lighter fluid to get the flames to a proper height....

MICHELLE
Are you crazy! You're not going to set me on fire!...

HUROK
Open your eyes toward Heaven, Michelle, and imagine that you are going to meet your Maker...or one of them....

MICHELLE
Stop him, Father... He's out of his mind....

CARDINAL CORDOBAS
I think I've seen enough to get the idea.

MICHELLE
In order to sell his film...a film that nobody wants.... He's actually
going to set me on fire!

CARDINAL CORDOBAS
Of course he isn't.... That would be going too far!

HUROK
(Adds more stuff to burn to the fire) You can accuse people in
Hollywood of anything....

MICHELLE
For heaven's sake, Father, stop him!

HUROK
Adultery, bigamy, sodomy, greed, back-stabbing,
plagiarism...anything but one.

MICHELLE
Get me out of here...I know what's going on....

HUROK
You can never accuse anyone in this town of ever going too far....

(HUROK breaks up a chair and adds the wood to the pile.)

HUROK
You don't have any matches on you, do you, Your Holiness?

MICHELLE
All that talk about having to be dead to be a saint....

HUROK
I've poured all my lighter fluid on the paper.

MICHELLE
You're going to burn me alive!

CARDINAL CORDOBAS
You're imagining things, my child....

MICHELLE
(Struggling) I'm not your child!

HUROK
Of course not. She's a child of destiny.

CARDINAL CORDOBAS
He wouldn't do that. I won't allow it!

HUROK
Just a little fire to get the juices flowing.... All actresses need that little touch of realism.... Remember Jean Seberg?

CARDINAL CORDOBAS
Untie her this instant!

HUROK
Don't touch her or I won't release her from her contract....

CARDINAL CORDOBAS
(Stops) What do you want from us?

MICHELLE
Josie! Help!

CARDINAL CORDOBAS
I can't speak for the pope....

HUROK
Let's go call him now, shall we?... And I can pick up some matches on the way back.

MICHELLE
I wouldn't play Joan of Arc if you were the last producer on the face of the earth!

HUROK
Doesn't she look exquisite.... Yes, I can see why the church has chosen her to be the first Saint of Cinema....

MICHELLE

Untie me, or I'm going to put your prick through a wine press!

(HUROK *and* CARDINAL CORDOBAS *go out. The great doors close behind them.* MICHELLE, *a lá Joan of Arc, remains tied to her stake.*)

MICHELLE

When I get through with you, you won't be fit for anything except for making love to flatworms....

(*As the lights dim, she leans the back of her head against the stake.*)

MICHELLE

Oh God...oh God...I never really wanted to be a saint.... All I ever wanted to be was the best damned baton twirler in Orange County.... But once the church calls you to be a saint, it's very difficult to say no.... (*Calls*) Josie, come here, this instant!... Josie!... And, for God's sake, put out your cigarette before opening the door!

(*Lights out*)

CURTAIN

CARWASH

CHARACTERS

KEN PFEIFFER
JOE WHISTLER
DARLENE SILVERMAN
YOUNG WOMAN

Originally published in *CrazyQuilt*, Vol. 4, No. 3 (September, 1989)

(In the dark we hear the sound of a carwash at full throttle.The water hums a powerful spray, the brushes create a concerto of scrub, the vacuum cleaners vacuum, pulling dust and dirt out of some kind of universe. The noise subsides. When the lights come on the Charm School Carwash, we see a few buckets of soap, large sponges, two or three folding chairs, dirty towels.)

(On stage are two men: KEN PFEIFFER, *who is dressed in a dark suit and who is carrying a briefcase, and* JOE WHISTLER, *a worker at the carwash.* JOE *is in simple work pants, sneakers, and a white shirt with the name:* CHARM SCHOOL CARWASH.*)*

PFEIFFER

Get me the manager!

JOE

I am the manager.

PFEIFFER

No, you're not the manager. You're a car thief.

JOE

Keep calm.

PFEIFFER

I am calm.

JOE

You're not calm.

PFEIFFER

You're not the manager!

JOE

I am one of the managers. Everyone on the lot is a manager. It's part of a new psychological theory for increasing profits. Make everybody feel the way the owner feels. We learned it from a book about the Japanese.

PFEIFFER

I don't want to hear about the Japanese right now.

JOE

Why? Are they ruining your business too?

PFEIFFER

I don't have a business. And, at the moment, I don't even have a car!

JOE

You have a car. You came in here with a car. You will leave with one.

PFEIFFER

I want to leave with the one I came in.

JOE

You will.

PFEIFFER

Where is it?

JOE

It has to be in there somewhere.

PFEIFFER

It's not in there. I keep telling you. It's not in there. Look!

(The owner of the carwash enters. She is DARLENE SILVERMAN. *In her mid-thirties, she is short, with frizzled hair. She wears a blue jumpsuit.)*

DARLENE

What seems to be the trouble here?

PFEIFFER

I want the manager.

DARLENE

I am the manager.

PFEIFFER

Of course. Everybody's a manager in this business. It's something you learned from the Japanese....

DARLENE

What's that supposed to mean?

JOE

He's upset because he lost his car.

DARLENE

He lost his car?

JOE

He lost his car.

PFEIFFER

I lost my car.

DARLENE

You lost your car?

PFEIFFER

What are we talking about here?

JOE

I thought we were talking about losing your car.

PFEIFFER

That's right. That's exactly what I'm talking about. Losing my car.

DARLENE

If you lost your car, what are you doing at a carwash? It doesn't make any sense to come to a carwash without any car.

PFEIFFER

Are you crazy? What are you talking about? I came here with my car. And now I don't have a car. I put it in there. *(Points to the carwash tunnel)*

DARLENE

(To JOE*)* What's he talking about?

JOE

He lost his car.

DARLENE

He lost his car?

PFEIFFER

I lost my car...in there.

DARLENE

Is this some kind of a joke? You lost your car in there?

PFEIFFER

I didn't lose the car. You lost the car.

DARLENE

(To JOE*)* What's he talking about? It's impossible to lose a car in there.

PFEIFFER

You did something to it.

JOE

I didn't touch the car.

PFEIFFER

Somebody touched the car!

JOE

I don't touch the cars until they come out of the tunnel. Yours didn't come out of the tunnel. Therefore, I didn't touch it.

DARLENE

(To PFEIFFER*)* See?

PFEIFFER

See what?

DARLENE

He didn't touch your car. So what are you complaining about?

PFEIFFER

What am I complaining about?

DARLENE

What are you complaining about?

JOE

What's he complaining about?

PFEIFFER

Stop it! I don't want you trying any of your charm school stuff on me.

JOE

What charm school stuff?

PFEIFFER

I don't find any of it charming.

DARLENE

I still don't understand what you're complaining about.

PFEIFFER

I told you.

DARLENE

You didn't tell me.

PFEIFFER

I drove my car into this Charm School and Carwash....

DARLENE

It's not charm school and carwash. It's Charm School Carwash. It's owned by a woman named Charm School.

PFEIFFER

There's actually a woman named Charm School?

DARLENE

Of course there is. You don't think that we would actually name a carwash Charm School unless the owner wanted her name upon it. But maybe you think it's funny to make fun of a person's name.

PFEIFFER

Are you the owner?

DARLENE

No, I'm the manager.

JOE

One of the managers.

DARLENE

My name's Darlene. This is Joe. What's your name?

PFEIFFER

Pfeiffer...Salten Pfeiffer.

DARLENE

Salten Pfeiffer and you make fun of someone named Charm School?

PFEIFFER

Don't do this to me!

DARLENE

Do what to you?

PFEIFFER

Put me on the defensive. It's you people who are at fault. Not me.
I drove my car in here in good faith. Put it on the conveyor belt,
got out, came over here, listened to the water, the brushes, and
waited for my car to emerge fully cleansed, brand-new, as it were....

JOE

And for less than two dollars too.

PFEIFFER

But my car didn't come out. What kind of a bargain is that?
The $80,000 car wash.

DARLENE

$80,000? What kind of car are you driving?

PFEIFFER

It was designed for a movie star.

DARLENE

Oh.

PFEIFFER

Oh? What do you mean by "oh"?

DARLENE

I mean you can't expect a movie star's car to act like everybody else's car.

PFEIFFER

I expect it to come out of a carwash.

DARLENE

Maybe it's still in there?

JOE

We looked. It's not in there.

PFEIFFER

What is this? The Bermuda Triangle? I bring my car in here and it goes up in a puff of smoke.

DARLENE

Smoke? Did you actually see a puff of smoke?

PFEIFFER

I didn't see anything. I have been waiting for my car to come out and it didn't come out.

DARLENE

Then why did you say a puff of smoke?

PFEIFFER

It was a figure of speech. A way of talking.

DARLENE

Well, don't say it if you don't mean it.

PFEIFFER

I mean it. I just don't believe it. What do you people do? Is it some kind of illusion? Some magician taught you to pluck people's cars out of thin air?

DARLENE

How do we know it happened?

PFEIFFER

What do you mean?

DARLENE

How do we know you actually came in here with a car?

PFEIFFER

Of course I came in here with a car. What else would I bring to a carwash. My laundry?...That's what I did. I brought you my underwear and called it a Mercedes.

DARLENE

No need to talk dirty.

PFEIFFER

I drove in here. I put my Mercedes on the conveyor belt. I got out.... The car went through and didn't emerge.

DARLENE

You can't prove it. I think you would actually have a difficult time proving you actually brought a car in here.

PFEIFFER

I don't have to prove it!

DARLENE

Of course you do. You don't think the owner is going to pay for a car that doesn't exist.

PFEIFFER

Of course it exists. I have it registered.

DARLENE

I mean exist here.

PFEIFFER

He saw me drive it in. *(To* JOE*)* Tell her you saw me drive it in.

JOE

I don't know. It was very busy at the time. A lot of cars were coming through.

PFEIFFER

Not an $80,000 silver Mercedes! What kind of a racket are you two running here?

JOE

Be careful what you say.

DARLENE

We're not running any racket. It seems to me that you're the one trying to cheat us.

JOE

How long do you think we could get away with stealing people's cars?

PFEIFFER

You're not stealing my car and getting away with it.

DARLENE

No one is stealing your car.

PFEIFFER

Get me another manager.

JOE

We're the only two.

PFEIFFER

Sorry. Somehow I had gotten the impression that everybody on this lot is a manager. It's a Japanese theory.

JOE

You're not a manager.

PFEIFFER

I'm not even the owner of my automobile anymore. I'm going to the police. This charm school is out of business.

DARLENE

Wait...tell me something.

PFEIFFER

I've been telling you something for the past twenty minutes, but nobody seems to be listening.

DARLENE

Just because we're not strong in communications theory, it doesn't
mean you have to yell at us.

PFEIFFER

I want my car back.

JOE

That we understand.

DARLENE

We want your car back too. Believe us. It doesn't help the reputation
of a carwash to be losing cars.

PFEIFFER

When it comes to reputation, you people are dead. Of course,
you can always change your name to Automobiles Anonymous.

DARLENE

It may not be our fault. It may be the manufacturer's fault.

PFEIFFER

How can it be the manufacturer's fault?

DARLENE

Have you ever had the car washed before?

PFEIFFER

What do you mean?

DARLENE

They're always recalling cars for something.

PFEIFFER

Not Mercedes! And not in the middle of a carwash. The
manufacturer didn't come in and pluck it right out of the tunnel.

DARLENE

I mean there might have been a glitch in the paint job. Some kind of
chemical so that if water is added to it, it just evaporates.

PFEIFFER

Mercedes don't evaporate. Buicks evaporate! Volkswagens!
Maybe even a Greyhound bus or two. But not an $80,000
custom-made Mercedes.

JOE

She's talking about the paint.

PFEIFFER

What? You don't think the car has been in the rain?

JOE

You have an $80,000 Mercedes and you leave it out in the rain.
You don't deserve a car like that.

PFEIFFER

Oh, I get it. You take it away from me because you think I don't
deserve it? Of all the carwashes in the United States, I have to pick
one that's Marxist....

DARLENE

Wait a minute, Mister. You're going too far.

PFEIFFER

I'm not going too far. I'm not going anywhere because I don't have
my car!

DARLENE

We didn't take away your car because you didn't deserve it.

PFEIFFER

Oh, really? Then just what was your motive for stealing my car?

JOE

We had no motive.

PFEIFFER

A bit cold-blooded, isn't it? To steal a valuable automobile without a
motive?

DARLENE

We didn't steal your car at all! What are you trying to do? Pull that old lawyer's stunt—"When did you stop beating your wife?"

PFEIFFER

You're lucky I'm not a lawyer.

DARLENE

You're lucky I'm not a lawyer.

PFEIFFER

Ah, but I know lawyers.

JOE

Don't look at me. I'm just the manager of a carwash.

DARLENE

Everybody knows a lawyer. It's nothing to be proud of.

PFEIFFER

But you're going to have the privilege of knowing my lawyers. We're going to sue you for everything you're worth.

DARLENE

We don't own the place.

JOE

And there are so many managers, we hardly manage it. Japanese theory only works if you have an emperor.

PFEIFFER

What a twentieth-century phenomenon: to absolve one's self of responsibility.

JOE

He should be a lawyer because I don't understand anything he's said nor anything that's happened. It's like a modern play.

PFEIFFER

You'll have plenty of time in jail to think about it.

DARLENE
We're not absolving ourselves of anything. Joe and I have been working at carwashes for years, but we have never lost a car yet.

JOE
(Sing-song) The cars go in,
The cars go out,
And all of us
Run about....

PFEIFFER
I don't see much running about here. In fact, I see very little heartfelt concern for my plight.

DARLENE
(Takes up a clipboard) I think that what has happened is so far out of the ordinary that we do not know how to cope with it.

PFEIFFER
Likely story. The extraordinary is easy to cope with; it's the ordinary that leaves everybody helpless.

DARLENE
Very well. We'll cope. What was the year of your car?

PFEIFFER
I don't understand.

DARLENE
Is it such a difficult question?

PFEIFFER
What? You have so many $80,000 Mercedes zipping through here, you think it got lost in the shuffle?

DARLENE
When we recover your automobile, we wish to be certain you get the right one.

PFEIFFER
You're stalling. You're playing for time.

DARLENE

Of course I am. Even as we talk, the molecules that we call automobiles might be reassembling themselves...and then we'll just turn around and there it will be.... *(She turns back to the carwash. The Mercedes has not appeared.)*

PFEIFFER

It's still not there.

JOE

Can I go home?

PFEIFFER

No. No one's leaving this lot until I get my car back.

DARLENE

What year was it?

PFEIFFER

Was? In the past tense already. That doesn't seem optimistic. Very well, it was a 1990.

JOE

1990?

DARLENE

Please don't joke. We have reputation to maintain.

PFEIFFER

I'm not joking. It's this year's model.

DARLENE

But this is 1989.

PFEIFFER

1990.

DARLENE

1989.

JOE

Do I get to vote?

PFEIFFER
A year is not a politician. It's not something you vote upon.

DARLENE
If we can't agree what year it is, how are we going to agree about getting your car back?

PFEIFFER
Please, Lord, don't let me be in a time warp!

JOE
What's a time warp?

PFEIFFER
What's a carwash?

DARLENE
Ontology is not our strong suit. Now may we continue with the business at hand?

PFEIFFER
It started out to be such a simple day. When I drove in here to wash my car, I really thought I had a handle on my life. I thought I had a clue to things.

JOE
It's television.

PFEIFFER
What's television?

JOE
Everything. Television is the reason that everything in life is going wrong.

PFEIFFER
That's a bit of a generalization, isn't it?

JOE
I'm just trying to be of help.

DARLENE
We watch old movies and lose our sense of time

PFEIFFER

I'm losing something, that's for certain. My car and my sense of time.
Perhaps I have been living a year ahead of everybody else.

JOE

Oh good.

PFEIFFER

What's good about it?

JOE

Series.You can tell me who's going to be in the World Series.

PFEIFFER

Who cares who's going to be in the World Series.

JOE

Well, who cares about losing a silly car?

PFEIFFER

Silly? A Mercedes silly? Religion is silly. War is silly. Selling
insurance is silly. But an $80,000 Mercedes is serious business.

JOE

There. You said it yourself. Why are you so upset about losing your
car when it's a material object completely covered by insurance?

PFEIFFER

I'm covered for theft, fire, and collision. I doubt if there is anything in
the policy about losing it in a carwash!

DARLENE

What about an act of God?

PFEIFFER

Ask Him, not me!

JOE

Who? Me?

PFEIFFER

No, God! If losing something in a carwash is an act of God, then I'd
hate to think how the pope discusses earthquakes.

JOE

Maybe that's it.

PFEIFFER

What's it?

JOE

Maybe while your Mercedes was being washed, there was an earthquake. The floor just opened up and swallowed the car.

PFEIFFER

In there?

JOE

In there.

PFEIFFER

Nowhere else all around us? Just in there, those few cubic feet where my Mercedes happened to be standing? Boom! And we didn't hear it? We didn't feel a thing?

JOE

It's possible.

PFEIFFER

Maybe a million ants left over from an old Charlton Heston movie crawled out of the jungles and climbed over the car and ate it!

DARLENE

No need to vent your sarcasm on us.

PFEIFFER

I'm not sarcastic. I'm insane. There's a difference. I've lost my mind.

DARLENE

Maybe the car is right in front of us, but we just can't see it.

JOE

See? There's the advantage of having more than one manager on the lot. It gives you a different perspective to the same problem. Those Japanese theories really work.

(DARLENE *gives* PFEIFFER *the clipboard.*)

DARLENE

Here. Hold this.

PFEIFFER

Why?

DARLENE

I'm going in there and get your car.

PFEIFFER

You're going in there and get my car?

DARLENE

I'm going in there and get your car.

JOE

I don't think I would go in there myself.

PFEIFFER

Don't stop her. If she thinks my car is in there, let her go get it.
Of course, if it's really in there, how she will get in there is more
than I know, because it is a law of physics: No two separate pieces
of matter can occupy the same place at the same time.

DARLENE

(*Pulls some wires out of the socket*) I'll just make certain everything is
unplugged.

JOE

No. Don't go in there.

PFEIFFER

It's only a carwash. Stop treating it like the Black Lagoon.

(*All three peer into the carwash.*)

JOE

We can see from this side all the way through to the other side. That
means there's nothing in there.

PFEIFFER

Oh.

JOE

She thinks she can find it.

DARLENE

I'll just walk in. If there's nothing there, then I'll emerge at the other side.

PFEIFFER

Sounds logical to me.

JOE

Let's all go together.

PFEIFFER

There is nothing to be frightened of. There's nothing in there.

DARLENE

I'll be right back.

PFEIFFER

One small natural law is broken and we go to pieces.

(DARLENE *enters the carwash.* JOE *and* PFEIFFER *watch her every move.*)

JOE

If it can happen once, it can happen again. And then we won't be able to trust anything ever.

PFEIFFER

(*To* DARLENE) Any clues?

JOE

We won't even be able to trust the law of gravity. Things will go flying off the earth.

PFEIFFER

No need to be melodramatic about it.

JOE

You're right. It's just a car. Why should the entire universe depend upon the appearance or disappearance of a single object?

PFEIFFER
I've always hated miracles...even when I was a little boy.

JOE
Darlene, do you see anything?

PFEIFFER
How can she see anything? There's nothing there to see.

JOE
Perhaps your Mercedes is of a very sophisticated design.
You can only see it when you're right on top of it.

PFEIFFER
Where is she?

JOE
Behind the big brushes?

PFEIFFER
No.

JOE
(Calls) Darlene!

PFEIFFER
She's gone!

JOE
She's not gone! Don't say that! Darlene!

PFEIFFER
If she's not gone, then where is she?

JOE
We count on the world acting a certain way and when it doesn't act
that way...Darlene!

PFEIFFER
I don't want to look.

JOE
I knew this was going to happen.

PFEIFFER

Happen! Are you crazy? Nobody could know it was going to.

JOE

I just knew it. I felt it.

PFEIFFER

Call the police.

JOE

Us? You think the police understand physics better than....

PFEIFFER

If you keep sending things through your carwash and they keep disappearing, you're going to lose your license.

JOE

Darlene isn't a thing....

PFEIFFER

Why didn't I go to the carwash down the street, the one recommended to me by my friends. All of this could have been avoided.

JOE

Your friends recommended the other carwash?

PFEIFFER

I didn't mean to offend you!

JOE

The other carwash is not run on sound business principles as set forth by the Japanese.

PFEIFFER

At least all their cars and managers don't disappear into thin air. Things go in and then they come out...usually clean...it makes for a clear profit margin.

JOE

How do you know? Maybe cars have been disappearing from
carwashes for years and everybody's been keeping silent about it....
Darlene!

PFEIFFER

She's not there. There's no sense to keep calling after her.

JOE

Where is she?

PFEIFFER

She's probably out somewhere riding around in my Mercedes.

JOE

She doesn't know how to drive

PFEIFFER

She shouldn't be practicing on my Mercedes somewhere in Never
Never Land.

JOE

Maybe it's like a black hole.

PFEIFFER

Then that is what it should be called—everything in the universe
should be correctly labeled.

JOE

Whatever is happening should not be happening. It's not right.

PFEIFFER

Black holes exist somewhere in outer space, not on the corner of Fifth
and Main.

JOE

I don't know.

PFEIFFER

Me neither.

JOE

Now what?

PFEIFFER
(Throws up his arms in despair) Got me.

JOE
I can't stand such an irrational universe.

PFEIFFER
I know.

JOE
I want things to make sense.

PFEIFFER
I know.

JOE
That's why books on corporate management, especially as written by the Japanese, make so much sense.

PFEIFFER
I never read one.

JOE
You should. You want me to lend you Darlene's? She's probably not coming back for it.

PFEIFFER
No, thanks.

JOE
Are you depressed?

PFEIFFER
Yes. Are you?

JOE
I don't know. It's weird. To watch a car disappear off the face of the earth should be the most wonderful thing that could happen, something beyond the ordinary, trivial events of the day....

PFEIFFER
You can say that...it's not your car....

DARLENE'S VOICE
(Calls from the carwash tunnel) Joe!... Mr Pfeiffer...are you there?

JOE
I'm here.... We're here.... Are you?

DARLENE'S VOICE
1 think I've got a clue....

JOE
What?

DARLENE'S VOICE
I think I've got a clue....

JOE
She says she thinks she has a clue.

PFEIFFER
I hear her, but I can't see her.

JOE
We're coming.

PFEIFFER
Wait a minute. You can't leave me here. I need you to substantiate my story....

(JOE disappears into the carwash.)

PFEIFFER
Hold on! Come back.... No one's going to believe me! *(He waits. No response. He peers into the carwash.)* Now what?

(He disappears into the tunnel. The lot is completely deserted. Then we hear the sound of a car horn from the street. It blasts two or three times, and then in comes a young woman in blouse, slacks, her hair tied under a bandanna.)

WOMAN
Hey, I would like to get my car washed. What happened to all the managers that used to be here? *(She peers into the carwash. She sees nothing.)* All right. I get the message. If you don't want my business, I can go elsewhere. This is not the only carwash in town. *(She walks off*

to her own car.) It's no way to run a business. A person could come in here and steal you blind. *(She's gone. The sound of a car starting.)* You've just lost a customer! *(Car drives away.)*

(Lights out)

CURTAIN

CONRAD ON THE VINE

CHARACTERS

JOSEPH CONRAD
MORRIS MALACHITE
LYDIA DUMARQUET
JOHN GARNETT

Scene One

(On stage, seated at a Victorian writing desk, is the great English novelist and short-story writer JOSEPH CONRAD. *He is impeccably dressed in a suit and cravat, and he is writing a letter to his friend Edward Garnett. The following is his actual letter, with the exception of the post script, of course, which allows us to drag the author, screaming and kicking, into the contemporary framework of our immaculate play.)*

CONRAD

(Reading his letter aloud)
Dear Edward,

Thank you for your letter. If I don't send proofs or type it is because there is, alas, so little to send and what there is, is not worthy. I feel it bad; and, unless, I am hopelessly morbid, I cannot be altogether wrong. So much I am conceited; I fancy I know a good thing when I see it. I am weary of the difficulty of it. The game is not worth the candle; of course, there is no question of throwing up the hands. It must be played out to the end but it is the other man who holds the trumps and the prospect is not inspiring.

I had letters about your Nietzsche from all sorts of people. You have stirred some brains! I don't think there is anything wrong with your wits. Galsworthy bought the *Outlook* the other day and began to read aloud from your Ibsen. He read a couple of paragraphs and asked, "Now who's this?" I said, "Garnett or the Devil". At that time I had no idea you wrote for that paper with the horrid caste-marks on its forepage. I am taking it now! You never tell me what you're doing.

Ever yours,

Conrad

P.S. Jessie sends her love and is in fair health. Oh, I almost forgot! I have been invited, through your kind suggestion I believe, to take part in the Morris Malachite Talk Show sometime within a fortnight.... It's on every morning and very popular. My publisher insists that it's a coup. He's sending a public relations man down to the studio to make the final arrangements. I shall keep you posted on the details.

(As he is finishing his postscript, lights down on CONRAD.*)*

(Lively talk-show music)

(Lights up on the television studio that houses the Morris Malachite Show. *[*CONRAD'*s writing desk becomes the desk where the noted talk-show host* MORRIS MALACHITE *sits.] There is a long white sofa, several spotlights, cue-cards, whatever says simply and economically that we are in a television studio. A long ropelike vine is suspended from the ceiling. From time to time, a studio worker will test its suitability by swinging in and then swinging out, without comment from anyone on stage, without anyone paying any attention.)*

(Enter MORRIS MALACHITE, *who is in his early fifties, with gray hair, and a well-manicured look. With him are his secretary,* LYDIA DUMARQUET, *in her thirties, trim and efficient, and* JOHN GARNETT, CONRAD'*s public relations man.)*

MORRIS MALACHITE

This show is going to be the highlight of the season. Just imagine, Joseph Conrad, Paul Tillich, Nolan Ryan, and Madonna going head to head to head to head on the topic DOES THE UNIVERSE EXIST? AND IF IT DOESN'T EXIST, SHOULD MORE NUDITY BE ENCOURAGED?

GARNETT

Yes, well...I just wish to be certain that Mr Conrad is comfortable. He is getting along in years, you know.

MORRIS MALACHITE

Yes, yes, we know. The first thing we ever learn about a writer is how far he or she is getting along in years. I suppose it provides them with the sanctity of wisdom.... Did you see my show on aging?

GARNETT

I'm sorry. I usually am at the publishing house early in the morning.

MORRIS MALACHITE

It was marvelous. Gore Vidal and Methusaleh. We got into orgasm and everything....

GARNETT

I don't think orgasm is a subject that Mr Conrad cares to discuss.

LYDIA

Is that Conrad with a C or a K?

GARNETT

He's English, not German.

MORRIS MALACHITE

I was under the impression he was Polish.

GARNETT

He was born Polish but he writes in English.

MORRIS MALACHITE

He writes in English? I didn't know that.

LYDIA

Am I given to undertstand the K is silent? *(Spells the name)* K-c-o-n-r-a-d?

GARNETT

There is no K.

LYDIA

Not anywhere?

MORRIS MALACHITE

(Leafing through one of CONRAD's *books)* I looked at the first page of his book and thought his work was in Polish.

GARNETT

(Crossing to get himself a cup of coffee from a tray, he ducks under a worker swinging on the vine.) A world without K's would be a strange world, wouldn't it? Where would Franz Kafka be?

MORRIS MALACHITE

Didn't we try to get Kafka on one of our shows, Lydia?

LYDIA

To discuss Sadomasochism and the Single Author.... But he was tied up.... I mean, he had a prior engagement.

MORRIS MALACHITE
(*Joining* GARNETT *at the coffee urn*) I try to get two or three writers on
every season. The trouble with writers, however, is that they like to
talk in complete sentences, and that's so tiring for the audience, you
know, having to follow a thought from one coordinating conjunction
to another. Please advise Mr Conrad to keep his comments brief.
We prefer the pithy and the anecdotal.

GARNETT
Could you give me some idea what kinds of questions you'll be
asking?

MORRIS MALACHITE
Certainly...Lydia, do you have the prompt list?

(LYDIA *takes a page or two from her clipboard.*)

LYDIA
We usually start with, "What do you think about having sex with
animals?"

GARNETT
Please cut that question.

MORRIS MALACHITE
You mean it's good enough for Madonna, but not good enough
for Joseph Conrad.... Let me tell you something, Madonna loves
answering that question. She wouldn't even come on the show if
we didn't ask it.

GARNETT
Mr Conrad won't appear if you do ask it.

LYDIA
If it's a language problem, we do have a translator assigned to him.

GARNETT
For what? Mr Conrad speaks English.

MORRIS MALACHITE
What kind of English does he speak?

GARNETT

What kind of English? English-English. The kind you and I are speaking.

MORRIS MALACHITE

Well, that's unfortunate. We were hoping he would speak Polish so we could have it translated. A foreign language adds a touch of class. Our audience just eats it up. And our advertisers love it, because the viewers at home have to read subtitles and that keeps them glued to the set for the commercials. It also allows us to talk about a lot of dirty stuff without the censors bothering us. Would Mr Conrad mind if he talked to us in Polish?

GARNETT

I don't think he's talked Polish for quite awhile.

MORRIS MALACHITE

It's all for a good cause.... See? We've got his book here. *The Heart of Darkness and Other Stories.* I'll hold it right up to the camera. We'll give it a good plug. You'll be astonished how many copies that will sell.... Especially if your author loosens up a bit and talks about the sex scenes.

GARNETT

Sex scenes? There are no sex scenes in *The Heart of Darkness.*

MORRIS MALACHITE

(Leafs through the book) No sex scenes in *The Heart of Darkness*? Are you certain?

GARNETT

Of course, I'm certain. My firm published the book.

MORRIS MALACHITE

Why would anyone want to publish a book without any sex scenes in it? Who would possibly buy it?

GARNETT

Now that's the kind of question you should be asking him: Why did he write the book? What kind of audience is he trying to reach? What mighty theme is he grappling with?

MORRIS MALACHITE

Any idiot can ask him those questions. My show is for living, breathing human beings.... Living, breathing human beings...they want to know what goes on after the lights go out. We're not giving college credit.... Look, you stay here and let my assistant go over the details with you. I have to go over a few details with my sound man.... It's been nice meeting you.

GARNETT

Well, I appreciate the exposure you are giving to my author's work.

(MORRIS MALACHITE *exits.*)

LYDIA

You look worried.

GARNETT

Well, to be frank about it, I am.

LYDIA

Morris has worked out something for him and it's very exciting.

GARNETT

That's what I'm afraid of.

LYDIA

You see this ropelike vine here?

GARNETT

Yes. I have been wondering what it was doing here.

LYDIA

This is for your Mr Conrad. He'll swing in on this vine, making jungle sounds. He drops down here right by the couch. Then he sits down.

(GARNETT *stares open-mouthed at her. He is, of course, speechless.*)

LYDIA

It's all right. It's perfectly safe.... It's not greased or anything. Look, I'll show you.

(LYDIA *goes off and returns, swinging on the vine. She makes appropriate animal cries. She swings off again. Returns. Swings off again. Finally, she drops down.*)

LYDIA

Is that an entrance or is that an entrance? It'll make headlines. Fleet Street will go out of its mind.

GARNETT

Please. I need to speak to Mr Malachite about this.

LYDIA

I'm afraid he's going to be tied up with the important guests.

GARNETT

(Seething) Get him for me right now.... I mean it...right this instant.

LYDIA

Well, if you feel that way about it.... Wait right here... *(Calls out)* Mr Malachite... *(Goes running off)* Mr Malachite!

(GARNETT *sits down and bangs his head against the desk several times.* LYDIA *and* MORRIS MALACHITE *immediately return.*)

MORRIS MALACHITE

Lydia says you are having some sort of minor problem?

GARNETT

You expect a writer of Conrad's international reputation to swing in on a vine?

MORRIS MALACHITE

Edith Sitwell would do it.

GARNETT

Screw Edith Sitwell!

MORRIS MALACHITE

At last an idea for a show! Even the B B C will go for it: THE SCREW EDITH SITWELL HOUR. Maybe we can get one of her brothers to sponsor it!

GARNETT

(Patting LYDIA's *arm)* Forgive me. It just slipped out.

LYDIA

That's okay Mr Garnett. I hear worse language around here
everyday.

MORRIS MALACHITE

I don't see the problem. Doesn't your author want to plug his book to
millions upon millions of potential buyers, or does he wish to spend
the rest of his life like the Hunchback of Notre Dame, bent over his
writing table, with nothing to show for his efforts but an electric light
bill of stunning proportions?

LYDIA

(Opening her briefcase) I think I know what's wrong, Mr Malachite.
I didn't get a chance to show him the costume.

MORRIS MALACHITE

Of course, that's the problem. It wouldn't make any sense for your
author to swing in all dressed up in his usual suit.... Lydia, show him
the costume.

*(*LYDIA *opens her briefcase and displays a costume fit for Tarzan.)*

LYDIA

There! Doesn't this make all the difference?

GARNETT

You expect Joseph Conrad to wear that?

MORRIS MALACHITE

Of course not, that one is too small for him. It was originally made
for Margaret Thatcher. We'll have one especially made for him.

GARNETT

It's Joseph Conrad you asked on your show. Not Tarzan.

MORRIS MALACHITE

I believe our viewers will be able to discern the difference.
Especially when we get to the philosophical part of it.

GARNETT

I suppose you want him to throw a spear at the same time?

MORRIS MALACHITE

Can he?... Lydia, see if we can find a pygmy to use as a target.

GARNETT

He's not going to throw a spear at any pygmy!

MORRIS MALACHITE

Of course. He wants a larger target.

GARNETT

He doesn't want any target!

LYDIA

Our attorneys will take care of the insurance problems.

GARNETT

Why would you want Mr Conrad to do this?

MORRIS MALACHITE

The Heart of Darkness is about Africa, isn't it?

GARNETT

It takes place in the Congo, yes.

MORRIS MALACHITE

Good. The blurb on the dust jacket was correct. See? It all falls into place.

GARNETT

Saying *The Heart of Darkness* is about Africa is like saying *The Scarlet Letter* is about the alphabet. Mr Conrad's book is about savagery. Exploring the dark side of British Imperialism.

MORRIS MALACHITE

That's exactly what we're saying.

GARNETT

Not in so many words.

MORRIS MALACHITE
Not in so many words, no. We deal in images. We're showing,
not telling.

GARNETT
I think you would prefer to have Tarzan on your show.If you want
Tarzan, get Tarzan....

LYDIA
We have him signed for our next show: Transexualism and Ape Men.

MORRIS MALACHITE
We call it: ME TARZAN, ME JANE.

GARNETT
Shall we do one show at a time? Joseph Conrad is not going to wear
that silly costume and swing in on a vine. That's all there is to it.

LYDIA
Try to think of it as a grand entrance.

GARNETT
Then let my author walk graciously (Demonstrating the entrance he
prefers) in like this and take his seat at this sofa like a gentleman.

MORRIS MALACHITE
We'll lose our audience.... When Sir Laurence Olivier walks on to a
stage, that's an entrance. When a writer walks in, it's not even a small
step for mankind. You can hear the audience groan and shudder
from here to Australia.... My way: Your writer swings in, dressed like
Tarzan, holding a copy of his book about Africa. I say it gets his book
on the best-seller list overnight. How do you think *Finnegan's Wake*
would have done if it hadn't been for our little send up in the hot tub?

GARNETT
You had James Joyce in a hot tub?

LYDIA
I was in there with him. Nude with two or three of my friends....
He swung in on this vine and just plopped in.

MORRIS MALACHITE
A good sport, Mr Joyce was.... Good sports sell books.

GARNETT
Mr Conrad is too old to be a good sport.

MORRIS MALACHITE
Well, that's that, is it?

GARNETT
That's that.

MORRIS MALACHITE
Why don't you just talk it over with him. Let your author make up his own mind.

GARNETT
I shall. But I know what he'll say.

MORRIS MALACHITE
As long as he says it in Polish. Well, come along, Lydia. Let's give Edith Sitwell a call.

(MORRIS MALACHITE *and* LYDIA *exit.* GARNETT *slumps down into the sofa. Lights down.*)

Scene Two

(*Music under. The theme music for the* Morris Malachite Show. *Lights quickly up on* CONRAD *and* GARNETT. CONRAD *is now dressed in the Tarzan outfit and carrying a long spear.*)

GARNETT
You're going through with this charade?

CONRAD
What choice do I have?

GARNETT
You can choose to say no.

CONRAD

Just say no. The simple-minded approach to the universe.... I'm sorry, John, I'm tired of sitting year after year at my writing desk and writing my heart out, my heart of darkness if you will, and no one caring.

GARNETT

Galsworthy cares.

CONRAD

Well, selling one book a year to Galsworthy is not going to feed my family.... Look at me, John, I have been writing for fifteen years and have never had a book sell more than a few thousand copies. At this rate, I'll end up like the Hunchback of Notre Dame with a huge gas and postage bill.

GARNETT

So Malachite and company used that argument on you too?

CONRAD

They didn't have to argue very hard when they pointed out what a brief appearance on the show will do for sales. Darwin's *Origin of the Species* would have gone completely unread if Darwin hadn't agreed to dress up in an ape costume and swing in on this very vine.

GARNETT

Suit yourself, but I'm not staying around to watch.

CONRAD

I don't know why you're complaining. It's your publishing house that will also benefit.

(As GARNETT *crosses out,* MORRIS MALACHITE *and* LYDIA *enter.)*

MORRIS MALACHITE

You look great, Mr Conrad. Just great. Now, my assistant Lydia will tell you when to climb on the vine and swing in. You drop down near the sofa, toss the spear at the little guy in the corner, and I'll hold up *The Heart of Darkness.* You got it?

CONRAD

I think so.

MORRIS MALACHITE

Good. Then I'll ask you a few questions about the African jungle and the place of man in the universe. But whatever I ask, it's important to keep your answers short because I've got three other guests, all opinionated. Very opinionated. That's the trouble with talk shows. Everybody wants to talk and everybody's got something to plug.

CONRAD

I thought I might read a statement from my preface to my novel, a few words about art and the artist.

MORRIS MALACHITE

Is it short?

CONRAD

A few sentences.

MORRIS MALACHITE

We might be able to work it in, but don't count on it. Prepared statements about art spell the death of art. This is a new world. Our audiences feast upon spontaneity, everything coming right off the top of our heads.... Now I've got to get in front of the curtain to warm up the old audience. I'll leave Lydia here with you in case you need anything...coffee, doughnuts, whatever. *(Going out)* It's going to work like a charm. Good thing you didn't listen to that friend of yours. Otherwise your book would end up in Nowheresville. *(He exits.)*

LYDIA

(Crossing to the sofa) It's important for writers to be good sports.

CONRAD

Do you know what question Mr Malachite is going start with?

LYDIA

I don't know. He likes to keep everybody on their toes. He likes to mix things up. It could range from anything from What do you think about sex with animals to How did all those years sailing on the sea influence your philosophy of life.

CONRAD

Mr Garnett hinted as much.

LYDIA

A very nice man, Mr Garnett.

CONRAD

A very nice man.

LYDIA

Didn't think too much of us, I don't think.

CONRAD

He's more at home in a different kind of world.

LYDIA

Aren't we all?... Do you want to practice your answers?

CONRAD

No, no. I have the answers written here. *(He gives her a typewritten slip of white paper.)* What I want is to practice swinging on that vine. I'm getting old and I don't want to fall off. Do I have time?

LYDIA

You might have the chance for just one quick swing in.

CONRAD

Good.

(CONRAD takes hold of the end of the vine and walks off with it.)

LYDIA

(Reads from the slip of paper the following sentences from the preface to The Nigger of the Narcissus*)* "...the artist appeals to that part of our being which is not dependent on wisdom; to that in us which is a gift and not an acquisition—and, therefore, more permanently enduring. He speaks to our capacity for delight and wonder, to the sense of mystery surrounding our lives; to our sense of pity, and beauty, and pain; to the latent feeling of fellowship with all creation—and to the subtle but invincible conviction of solidarity that knits together the loneliness of innumerable hearts, to the solidarity in dreams, in joy, in sorrow, in aspirations, in illusions, in hope, in fear, which binds men to each other, which binds together all humanity—the dead to the living and the living to the unborn."

(As she reaches the final word, CONRAD, *with a Tarzan-like yell, swings in on his vine.)*

(Lights out)

CURTAIN

ETHIOPIA

CHARACTERS

MAN
WOMAN
WAITER
FATHER
MOTHER
DAUGHTER
SON

(The stage consists of a set of bleachers that are placed upstage facing the audience. Downstage center is a round table set for elegant dining—white tablecloth, silver utensils, flowers, candles, violin music. At the table are a MAN and a WOMAN in formal dress, who are partaking in a lobster and caviar feast. Enter the WAITER in black tie. He checks with the couple about the wine list. Enter the Macabee family: FATHER, MOTHER, DAUGHTER aged sixteen, SON aged eleven. The WAITER, seeing the Macabee family enter, rushes to them to keep them from entering the dining area. They are certainly not in formal evening attire. Nor are they in rags. The FATHER wears a sports jacket and tie, the MOTHER a simple dress and jacket, the children their school clothes.)

WAITER

You have tickets, I presume.

FATHER

Tickets...oh, yes, the tickets. *(He searches his pockets.)* Who has the tickets. Mother, did I give you the tickets?

SON

I have the tickets, Pop.

MOTHER

Give the tickets to the gentleman, William.

(SON holds out the tickets. WAITER takes them, scrutinizes them, gives the family a cold stare.)

WAITER

You are early.

FATHER

I know, but we had a long way to come.

MOTHER

We tried to leave in plenty of time so we wouldn't be late.

WAITER

These tickets are only good for the dessert portion.

SON

See, Pop, didn't I tell you? It says dessert right on the tickets.

MOTHER

Quiet, William. Let your father handle this. He's paying for it.

DAUGHTER

I'm so humiliated.

MOTHER

(To DAUGHTER*)* Not another word out of you, young lady.

(As the music fades away, the audience becomes aware of a certain chanting or recitation of the names of the cities and towns of Ethiopia. They need not be recited in alphabetical order. The names of the cities and towns should provide a steady texturing of background noise that filters in and out with the violin music.)

OFF-STAGE RECITATION

Addis Ababa, Addis Alam, Adola, Aduwa, Agordat, Aksum, Ankober, Arba Mench, Asmara, Assab, Asselle, Awareh, Awash, Bako, Bedessa, Burei, Burye, Challafo, Chilga, Dagabur, Dallol, Dangila, Debra Birhan, Debra Markos, Debra Tabor, Dembidollo, Dessye, Dilla, Dire Dawa, Dolo, Domo, Edd, El Carre, El Der, Filtu, Gabredarre, Galadi, Gambela, Gedo, Gerlogubi, Goba, Gondar, Gore, Gorrahei, Hadama, Harar, Harkiko, Hosseina, Jijiga, Jimma, Keren, Koma, Lalibela, Magdala, Maji, Makale, Massawa, Masslo, Mega, Mendo, Mersa Fatma, Metamma, Miesso, Murle, Mustahil, Nakamti, Nakfa, Nejo, Saio, Soddi, Sokota, Tessenei, Thio, Tori, Umm Hajar, Waka, Wadia, Wardere, Wota, Yabalio, Yirga-Alam, Zula.

FATHER

I really don't see anyone else in the bleachers.

(The diners never pay any attention to the spectators.)

WAITER

That is beside the point, isn't it?

FATHER

I suppose so...perhaps.

DAUGHTER

I could die.

MOTHER

You will, young lady, if you don't stand still and keep quiet.

WAITER

If you please return at the proper time, I shall be happy to seat you.

SON

Pop, what does dessert mean? You told me, but I forgot.

(FATHER, *pulling out his wallet, ignores* SON's *question.*)

FATHER

Let me just pay a little extra and maybe we could be seated now?

(WAITER *stares at* FATHER *with contempt.*)

FATHER

We've come such a long way.

DAUGHTER

I wish I were dead.

(FATHER *gives* WAITER *a fifty-dollar bill.*)

WAITER

Very well. But don't show your tickets to anyone.

FATHER

We won't.

WAITER

Under no circumstances are you to disturb the diners.

FATHER

We understand that.

WAITER

After all, they have paid a lot more than you.

(WAITER shows the family its seats in the bleachers. Way up back. Far away from the diners.)

WAITER

If anyone else arrives for the main course you may have to relinquish your seats.

FATHER

I understand.

DAUGHTER

If anyone else comes I will kill myself.

MOTHER

I wish you would stop talking like that, young lady. It is absolutely unbecoming.

WAITER

You have all taken your hunger suppressant pills?

FATHER

Of course.

WAITER

Good. *(He turns to go.)*

FATHER

One more thing...

WAITER

What now?

FATHER

Do you have a program?

WAITER

Program?

FATHER

Something to understand what we're watching?

WAITER

What you're watching?

FATHER

Well, you know...it's been a long time....

(FATHER *gives* WAITER *another fifty-dollar bill.*)

WAITER

Oh, you mean a menu?

FATHER

Yes, a menu...I guess that's what I mean.

WAITER

Very well, I can bring you a menu to share.... But please don't slobber all over it. Or chew it. *(He goes down the bleachers to fetch a fancy, red, bound menu.)*

WAITER

Or nibble. *(He exits.)*

SON

Boy, Pop, we're really spending the loot tonight. Aren't we?

MOTHER

Well, William, you should feel very fortunate. Not everyone can sit here and see all this.

SON

All what? What are they doing?

DAUGHTER

I could have stayed home.

FATHER

We don't know what they're doing until we get the menu.

(WAITER *has returned with the menu. He presents it to* FATHER, *opens it for him. Exits.*)

SON

I'm going to move down, closer to the action.

FATHER

No, you're not.

SON

Yes, I am.

FATHER

Just wait a few minutes. We don't want to get into any trouble.

SON

Trouble? What kind of trouble? There's no one else sitting here.

MOTHER

Please, William! Don't give us a difficult time tonight. We've gone to considerable sacrifice to make this evening possible. Not many people get to watch other people eat.

SON

Big deal!

MOTHER

Well, you'll think better of it when you're the envy of everybody at school tomorrow.

DAUGHTER

I'd die before I'd tell anybody what we're doing.

FATHER

(Studying the menu) Look at that. They're eating real caviar.

DAUGHTER

We were only supposed to come for the dessert.

FATHER

Well, now we're going to see more!

MOTHER

They're eating real caviar.

SON

What's caviar?

FATHER

I don't know.

SON
Then how do you know what they're eating?

FATHER
Because it's what it says here.

DAUGHTER
He's reading it off the menu, stupid.

MOTHER
Fish eggs.

FATHER
What? *(To* DAUGHTER*)* What did your mother say?

MOTHER
Fish eggs.

DAUGHTER
Fish eggs. Mother said fish eggs.

FATHER
Well, you just can't sit there and say fish eggs. Just like that.
People will laugh.

MOTHER
I think caviar is fish eggs.

FATHER
Really?

SON
Mom has gone off her rocker.

FATHER
I guess they're eating fish eggs, Son.

SON
Why?

FATHER
I don't know.

MOTHER

At least it's real food.

DAUGHTER

I'd rather have the pill.

SON

Well, everyone knows what pill you're on.

DAUGHTER

Mother!

MOTHER

Stop it, you two, this instant, or we won't bring you here again.

FATHER

It's an idle threat. There's no way we'll be able to come back here again.... Not at these prices.

SON

Will someone tell me what eating is?

FATHER

Can't you see? It's what those people are doing.

MOTHER

It's not his fault, Father. He doesn't know any better.

DAUGHTER

It's disgusting.

FATHER

You put food in your mouth and you chew and you chew and you chew and then the food goes down to your stomach where it's digested.

SON

Seems like a lot of wasted energy.

FATHER

I suppose it does.

DAUGHTER
What's that stuff in their hands?

FATHER
Bread.

MOTHER
It could be steak.

FATHER
It's bread. I've seen pictures.

SON
How come I haven't seen pictures of bread?

MOTHER
You're too young.

DAUGHTER
(To SON*)* I bet there's pictures of bread in those dirty magazines you have.

OFF-STAGE RECITATION
Addis Ababa, Addis Alam, Adola, Aduwa, Agordat, Aksum, Ankober, Arba Mench, Asmara, Assab, Asselle. Awareh, Awash, Bako, Bedessa, Burei, Burye, Challafo, Chilga, Dagabur, Dallol, Dangila, Debra Birhan, Debra Markos, Debra Tabor, Dembidollo, Dessye, Dilla, Dire, Dawa...

SON
I don't know what you're talking about.

DAUGHTER
All those dirty magazines have fold-outs of some kind of foodstuff.

MOTHER
And just how would you know, young lady?

DAUGHTER
Because somebody told me about it. Staples right in the belly of something called pudding.

*(*WAITER *enters.)*

OFF-STAGE RECITATION

Dolo, Domo, Edd, El Carre, El Der, Filti, Gabredarre, Galadi, Gambela, Gedo, Gerlogubi...

WAITER

Really! This is impossible.

FATHER

They're eating caviar, aren't they?... And that's bread?

WAITER

That's none of your business. It's written in the contract, and I told you myself.... You cannot disturb the diners.

FATHER

(Feebly) I paid good money for these seats.

SON

That's right, Pop! You tell him.

WAITER

Are you going to leave peaceably, or am I going to have to call the authorities?

MOTHER

My husband was merely trying to explain to our children what was going on.

WAITER

The diners must not be disturbed!

(The male diner drops a small piece of bread. It falls to the floor.)

SON

Pop, the man dropped a piece of bread.

WAITER

Really! You people have left me no choice!

(SON scampers down the bleachers in search of the piece of bread.)

MOTHER

Will, come back here.

WAITER
Young man!

DAUGHTER
Mother, didn't I tell you this would happen?

FATHER
Son!

OFF-STAGE RECITATION
Hadama, Harar, Harkiko, Hosseina, Jijiga, Jimma, Gore, Gorrehei,
Koma, Lalibela, Magdala, Maji, Makale, Massawa, Masslo, Mega,
Mendo, Mersa Fatma, Metamma, Miesso, Murle, Mustahil, Nakamti,
Nakfa, Nejo, Saio, Soddi, Sokota, Tessenei, Thio, Tori, Umm Hajar,
Waka...

(SON dives under the velvet ropes and hurls himself onto the crust of bread.)

FATHER
Don't touch their food!

(The two diners stand up. They stare at the family and WAITER.)

MAN
He's touched the food!

(The two diners turn on their heels and walk off in different directions.)

WAITER
(To the family) You know the penalty!

MOTHER
It's our first time here. We didn't know.

FATHER
Come back here, Will. I mean it.... Right now.

*(SON stands up and slowly returns to the bleachers. The bread remains
where it has fallen. The rest of the food remains upon the table.)*

WAITER
I am going for the authorities. You know the penalties.

DAUGHTER
What did it feel like? What did the bread feel like?

MOTHER

Margaret!

FATHER

(To WAITER*)* I have more money.... Let me give you money....

*(*WAITER *has gone. The family gathers around* SON *and they embrace.)*

DAUGHTER

Dirty? Just like in the magazines?

MOTHER

(To SON*)* Why did you have to touch the food?... Why?

OFF-STAGE RECITATION

Nafka, Sokota, Tessenei, Harkikio, Hadama, Gore, Koma....

(Lights out)

CURTAIN

THE MAN WHO
ATE EINSTEIN'S
BRAIN

CHARACTERS

Dr Kilgaroff Moran
Jeremiah Samuel Goldberg
Dr Steiner

(We are in the laboratories of the famed brain surgeon Dr Kilgaroff
Moran. *This laboratory may be as elaborate or as sparse as the set budget
allows. On the table are a large empty bottle, a plate, some knives, forks, a
bowl of soup, etc. A few test tubes. A refrigerator. A small writing desk with
a rolling chair. The lab grows more complex the further we go into it.)*

(Working away is Jeremiah Samuel Goldberg, *the janitor. He is an old
man with white hair and moustache. He is seated at the counter and is
finishing off his bowl of soup. In front of him are several Polaroid photos.)*

*(*Dr Moran *enters. He is a tall, slender redhead in a lab coat. He is pulling
off his surgical mask and gloves. He picks up a photo.)*

Dr Moran

New photos of Elise and Kinsey at work, I see. *(He crosses to a shelf of
bottles. Searches for something. Turns back to the empty bottle. He gasps.)*

Goldberg

Anything wrong, Doctor?

Dr Moran

This bottle's empty. This bottle, which was supposed to be kept
under lock and key at all times, is standing out in the open.
(Checks the notebooks) Did one of my assistants put the contents
somewhere else? *(He crosses to a refrigerator and opens it. It is only
stocked with beer, a dead sheep, and otter droppings.)* Nope. Just the
usual. Beer, a dead sheep, and otter droppings.... Goldberg, sound
the alarm! Some one has stolen Einstein's brain!

Goldberg

Someone has stolen Einstein's brain? *(Calls out)* Sound the alarm!

*(*Dr Moran *covers the janitor's mouth.)*

Dr Moran

Sam, I'm sorry! Don't sound the alarm! If word of this loss gets out,
I'm ruined. A lifetime of research will go down the drain. No one
will trust this lab to preserve scientific treasures again. We shall

become known only as the otter droppings and dead sheep capital of neuroresearch. *(Releases* GOLDBERG*)* Not a word to anyone, Goldberg, or this lab will become the laughingstock of the scientific community. That is, if we dare call such an enclave of money-grubbing, servile, back-stabbing, envious seekers of personal glory a community.

GOLDBERG

I won't tell a soul.

DR MORAN

Every doctoral candidate will be out to get me. I shall be known as the butterfingers of neurosurgery. The man who allowed Einstein's brains to slip through his fingers!

GOLDBERG

I wouldn't put it that way, Doctor.

DR MORAN

Look at me. My hands are shaking, I'm coming from surgery. Hours spent trying to cram a filagree of taste into the skull of a rock musician.... I thought I would relax by retreating here for a few hours of close scrutiny of Einstein's brain cells, dance once around the block with endoplasmic reticula.... But look! The bottle is empty.... Why were Einstein's brains treated so cavalierly?

GOLDBERG

Pardon me, Dr Moran, but why would Einstein's brain be kept in a bottle?

DR MORAN

(Searching through cabinets) And why shouldn't Einstein's brain be in a bottle—that's the question to ask. Where would you keep the brains of the greatest genius of the twentieth century? In a postcard album? Maybe dangle them over the dashboard of a car? According to the dictates of Einstein's will, moments after Einstein's death, my colleagues and I were given permission to cut open Einstein's skull, remove his brain, and preserve it for study. This my miserable colleagues and I did. Each year, one of us would have exclusive domain over the greatest scientific property of our time. This year is my year. My year! It might as well have been the year of the bubonic plague. This is terrible. This is the worst thing that has ever happened to my laboratory since it opened nineteen years ago.... Dr

Moran's Deli and Brain Surgery.... Listen to me. I'm babbling....
What will happen to my research grant now, I ask you. No money's
flowing into the coffers.... It's sabotage, I tell you. Deliberate
sabotage. Dr Kinsey did this. Kinsey has always been jealous of
my work. Was Dr Albert Kinsey in here today?

GOLDBERG

I thought Dr Kinsey was conducting sex research.

DR MORAN

Yes, Kinsey's into sex...who isn't? But, secretly, he really wanted to
play with another organ. The human brain. The greatest sex organ of
them all. And who would have the dirtiest thoughts of all? Einstein
of course. That's it! Kinsey made off with the brain to further his
research into sexual fantasies....

GOLDBERG

I don't think so, Doctor.

DR MORAN

Of course you don't think so, Sam. You've been a widower for nearly
a decade. You've forgotten these things. But Kinsey's out there, his
telescope trained into every bedroom window of this fair land. For
that he gets paid, while my career languishes in the backwaters of
grantsmanship. I deserve a break.

GOLDBERG

I meant Einstein's brain.

DR MORAN

Sam, I can tell by the way you're leaning on your broom, you know
more than you're letting on.... Tell me, before I go mad. What do you
know?

GOLDBERG

I think I ate it.

DR MORAN

I think I have gone mad. Children making faces at
me—"nayanaanhaya. You're the man who lost Einstein's brain."

GOLDBERG

God forgive me, Dr Moran. I think I ate Einstein's brain.

DR MORAN

You think you ate Einstein's brain.... Well that's all right. If you just think you did. Thinking is not the same thing as doing. Only a high-strung theologian would say otherwise.

GOLDBERG

(*Holds up a soup bowl*) See the little graymatter floating in this bowl?

DR MORAN

Don't tell me.

GOLDBERG

I thought you wanted to know.

DR MORAN

I wanted to know, but I didn't want to know that.... No, I wanted to know something else entirely actually....

GOLDBERG

It tasted like chicken.

DR MORAN

Einstein's brain tasted like chicken? Is there no justice? Einstein's brain should taste like truffles en brouchette!

GOLDBERG

I'm a simple man with simple tastes, Sir.

DR MORAN

Now I know you're jesting. Brains are not kosher, Goldberg! If lobsters are out of bounds, think how God feels about digging into human skulls for lunchtime snacks?

GOLDBERG

I thought it was a matzoh ball. A very large and soggy matzoh ball.

DR MORAN

A matzoh ball?

GOLDBERG

I admit it didn't taste like a matzoh ball.

DR MORAN

Of course not. The brain after all had been preserved in formaldahyde. I can't imagine what it tasted like.

(GOLDBERG *hands him the soup bowl. Then a spoon.*)

GOLDBERG

You try it. See what it tastes like to you.

(DR MORAN *looks at the gray stuff floating in the bowl.*)

DR MORAN

My God, that looks like human brain tissue floating in there....
What's the yellow stuff?

GOLDBERG

I told you. It didn't taste right so I added a can of chicken soup to it.

DR MORAN

No wonder the brain tasted like chicken.

GOLDBERG

That makes sense, now that I think of it.

DR MORAN

Science thrives on simple explanations, the most elegant of solutions
to complex problems.... *(Exploding)* You idiot!

(DR MORAN *grabs* GOLDBERG *by the throat, pushes his head back to the
top of one of the counters, and starts choking him.*)

DR MORAN

You and your craving for lunch have ruined the greatest scientific
experiment of the twentieth century....

GOLDBERG

Please, Doctor, I can't breathe....

(DR STEINER *enters the lab. She is a tall, twenty-six-year-old brand-new
P h D, willowy blonde in a lab coat.*)

DR MORAN

I can't breathe either. After what you have done. The whole civilized world won't be able to breathe.... Everything is ruined.

DR STEINER

Dr Moran! Stop it! What are you doing?

(She manages to disengage DR MORAN *from* GOLDBERG's *throat.)*

DR MORAN

Why is it that everybody who enters this lab is always asking me what I am doing? Can't I have a few secrets to myself?

DR STEINER

You were trying to choke Sam. I saw you. If I hadn't entered the room when I had, poor Sam would be dead.

DR MORAN

(Trying to regain his composure) Nonsense. I was merely conducting a simple, basic scientific experiment.

GOLDBERG

(Hoarsely) Wasser.

DR MORAN

I wanted to see if air cut off from the brain would cause any significant damage to a common criminal.

DR STEINER

What are you talking about? Sam has been working here for twenty years. He's no criminal.

GOLDBERG

(A dazed expression on his face) I'm a genius actually. I am beginning to experience deep insights into theoretical physics.

DR STEINER

What are you talking about, Sam? You don't know anything about theoretical physics.

GOLDBERG

Well, you see, there is the simple theory of relativity and then there's the complex theory of relativity. Let's use the analogy of riding on a train that is going faster than the speed of light.

DR MORAN

Not bad for an old man who doesn't know the difference between a quark and a handball court.

GOLDBERG

(In German) Beim Mittagessen habe Ich das Gehirn Einsteins gefressen. Das war ja ein Irrtum. Ein Missverstandnis.

DR MORAN

What did he say?

DR STEINER

He said that by mistake he ate Einstein's brain for lunch.... Sam, I didn't know you spoke German.

GOLDBERG

(In German) Leider noch nicht. Denn Ich habe nie in meinem Leben Deutsch gesprochen.

DR STEINER

But you're speaking to us in German now.

DR MORAN

Don't you believe it, Dr Steiner. Just as all strange meats taste like chicken, all strange tongues sound like German.

GOLDBERG

(In German) Wo habe Ich meine Geige Verlagt.

DR STEINER

Sam, you don't play the violin.... Dr Moran, won't you explain?

DR MORAN

Explain?

DR STEINER

Yes. Explain.

DR MORAN

Frankly, I don't have any explanations. I find it astonishing that I have gotten this far.

DR STEINER

You're crazy. Both of you.

DR MORAN

That may be, but one of us is crazy with another man's brain in his belly.

DR STEINER

I see that the bottle that held Einstein's brain is empty.

DR MORAN

What did you expect?

(GOLDBERG *heads out.*)

DR MORAN

Sam! Where are you going?

GOLDBERG

Don't worry, Doctor. I'll be right back. I have a sudden need to play the violin. *(He exits.)*

DR STEINER

Dr Moran, what have you done with Einstein's brain? It was supposed to be in this bottle, and the bottle is supposed to be kept under lock and key at all times.

DR MORAN

Opening a laboratory door is a metaphor representing a new sphere of discovery.

DR STEINER

(Checking the log book) Nothing in the log book. No one has signed it out.

DR MORAN

As you can see, the last person to sign anything out was your fiancé, Dr Kinsey.... He signed out Elise, our twenty-one-year-old graduate assistant.... Opening bedroom doors is a metaphor for what some others of us do.

DR STEINER
If I catch Albert with Elise, I shall kill him.

DR MORAN
Please, Dr Steiner. Jealousy has no place in the sciences...with the exception of biology, perhaps. Any science that bases its reputation upon the dissection of frogs can only come to a bad end.... What's wrong with me? I see my career crashing into a black hole. A vacuum of ridicule.

DR STEINER
Has someone removed Einstein's brain from our lab without permission?

DR MORAN
Not exactly.

DR STEINER
What do you mean "not exactly"?

DR MORAN
I mean that language is so abstract that it is extremely difficult to say anything exactly in it. Yes, that is exactly what I mean to say...in an inexact manner, of course.

DR STEINER
Dr Moran, you're babbling!
(GOLDBERG returns, bearing a violin case.)

DR MORAN
That's exactly the problem with language, isn't it? As soon as a person steps out into the deep end of the linguistic pool, what appears to be shallowness sets in.

GOLDBERG
(In Chinese) Wo ch'ih la.

DR STEINER
Now Sam is speaking Chinese.

DR MORAN
Don't pay any attention. He's just showing off.

DR STEINER
He said he ate it.

(GOLDBERG *takes out the violin and begins to play.*)

DR MORAN
(Puts out a tape recorder) Sam, for the sake of our experiment, let's stick to German. It's academically acceptable, and we don't have to translate.

DR STEINER
Our experiment? What experiment?

DR MORAN
(Opening the refrigerator) Where's the aspirin? There used to be a bottle behind the dead sheep.... I have an idea!... By George, I've got it!

GOLDBERG
(Sings) Je l'ai mange.

DR MORAN
Dr Steiner, sit down. I shall tell you exactly what happened. I got tired with all the piddling, plodding little experiments being done with Einstein's brain and so, taking the world upon my shoulders, I took the great plunge. I fed Einstein's brain to an ordinary janitor and see the results? The man now thinks with that additional brain. I have created a new genius....Take notes, take notes...we'll write this up for *Cell* magazine...and I shall make a name for myself.... What a genius I am.... Actually, I take it back....What a genius he is.... What geniuses we all are!

DR STEINER
(To GOLDBERG*)* Did you really eat Einstein's brain?

GOLDBERG
Ja...Ich habe das Gehirn Einsteins gefressen.

DR MORAN
Go ahead. Ask him what he's done.

DR STEINER

I will not!... Are you mad? Both of you.

DR MORAN

Dr Steiner, please keep calm. Sit down here and think back to the thrilling days of yesteryear, the sound of hooves, and the mighty cry of "Hi Ho Silver!"... Do you remember the experiments conducted on earthworms? You teach one earthworm to crawl through a maze. Then you cut up its body into tiny pieces and feed them to other earthworms, and all those newly fed earthworms can navigate the same maze without ever having seen it before? I have merely turned the experiment up a notch. Two or three notches, in fact. Hell! I've turned it all the way up!

DR STEINER

You cut up Einstein's brain and fed the pieces to Sam?

GOLDBERG

Bitte, ich hoffe ich store nicht....

DR MORAN

(He will not be contradicted.) Silence, you hun!... Go back to your violin playing.

GOLDBERG

Mir steigen Gleichungen auf vor meinem geistigen Augen...ich mochte sie niederschreiben.

DR MORAN

What did he say?

DR STEINER

He says he sees equations floating in front of his eyes and he wants to write them down.

DR MORAN

(Opening a desk drawer) Quick!... Pencil, papers, notebook...ink, erasers. (He brings GOLDBERG writing implements.) Perhaps you wish to sit at the computer.... No, no, I know. You're elegant. Years of thinking and then a few notes upon a piece of paper.... Do you prefer lined or unlined?

(GOLDBERG *sits down at a small desk. We can hear the scratch of his pen across paper.*)

DR STEINER

This is all too extraordinary to believe.

DR MORAN

It's up to us, working together, to make it believable. We'll write this up for the journals and stand back to allow the grant monies to flow in. We'll be standing up to our asses in filthy lucre. I'll be back on the top of the heap again! Think of the good work we'll be able to do.

DR STEINER

I don't think it's a good idea to rush into print with this experiment, do you?

DR MORAN

Rush? (*Looks at his watch*) What's the rush?

DR STEINER

Well, how long have you been working on it? It couldn't be very long.

DR MORAN

How long? (*Looks at his watch again*) Let me think...twenty years.

DR STEINER

That's impossible! Einstein's brain was in the bottle yesterday. I saw it myself.

DR MORAN

Time is relative, my dear. It goes faster for me than it does for you. That's why men and women have such problems with sex.... Besides, it is not the length of time. You know that. It's the truth of the insight. One day you're sitting under an apple tree, and the next moment a dead sheep drops off a limb—and voila! Gravity! The way I see it, next we cut up Goldberg's brain here...feed it to others and so on and so on and soon we shall have a world of persons with Einstein's capabilities....

(*In a frenzy of creative mathematics,* GOLDBERG *is scribbling madly, tossing papers this way and that.*)

DR STEINER

Cell magazine may not take kindly to publishing an experiment that requires participants to slaughter innocent victims and then eat their brains.

DR MORAN

Very well. We'll try for *Playboy* first....

DR STEINER

I'm going to be sick.

DR MORAN

Experimental science, like minimalist painting, is not for the squeamish....

GOLDBERG

(Bursts into a recitation) "Ich hatte selbst oft grillenhafte Stunden, Doch solchen Trieb hab' ich noch nie empfunden."

DR MORAN

What's he saying?

DR STEINER

I believe he's reciting Goethe.

DR MORAN

That's not going to help. Concentrate, Sam!. *(He paces.)* Let me see... *(Talks into his dictaphone)* A few bites of Einstein's brain and our hard-working janitor...no, let's use the word laboratory custodian... and he burst into reciting German poetry, playing the violin, and writing down mathematical equations, activities for which he had never evidenced any prior interest or talent.

GOLDBERG

"Das ist die Welt."

DR MORAN

Quiet, kraut-head. Can't you see I am working on a breakthrough paper? Three hours after digesting Einstein's brain, Mr Jeremiah Samuel Goldberg began to work on a series of equations which may lead us to a unified view of the universe.

DR STEINER

That's not true! Look what Sam's written: 12 + 12 = 5. 2 + 7 = 18. 4 x 5 + 2 =...he's blotted the last answer out.

DR MORAN

(*Studies the papers*) Oh Sam, I am so disappointed in you. You could do so much better.... All right, we'll lift some equations from Einstein's early work and say that Sam spontaneously came up with them on his own.... Both of us shall have to practice Sam's handwriting.

DR STEINER

(*Genuinely shocked*) Fake the evidence?

DR MORAN

Dr Steiner, quit looking so shocked. Some scientists view experimental science one way; some scientists another. Making facts up...what can be more experimental than that?... It should be obvious to you what Sam had wanted to do. The great equations are still locked upstairs in his head. It's up to us to unlock them.

DR STEINER

You can't see what's going on in his head.

DR MORAN

But I'm the world's authority on the human brain. Who are they going to believe? Me? Or some baggy-pants laboratory custodian?

GOLDBERG

Can I go to the bathroom?

DR MORAN

What? And eliminate Einstein's brains from your system? No! Of course not. Sit down and think of something else.

GOLDBERG

You mean I can never go to the bathroom again?

DR MORAN

Say something intelligent about the need for world peace.

DR STEINER
Surely, Dr Moran, you can't be that inhuman.

DR MORAN
(Opening cabinets) Are you implying world peace is inhuman?

DR STEINER
I'm not talking about world peace. I'm talking about Sam.

DR MORAN
From now on we shall refer to him as Einstein II.

GOLDBERG
(Quoting Einstein) "Where the world ceases to be the scene of our personal hopes and wishes, where we face it as free beings admiring, asking, and observing. There we enter the realm of art and science."

DR MORAN
Much better, Sam.

GOLDBERG
I have a sudden desire to smoke a pipe.... Can I get a pipe?

DR MORAN
All right, but hurry back... We have important work to do. You have to write some letters to Freud.... Maybe a protest against the atomic bomb.

(GOLDBERG exits.)

DR MORAN
(Calls after him) And don't go to the bathroom!... *(Back to* DR STEINER*)* Now, let's begin our paper. *(Starts to write)* "It was a dark and stormy night."

DR STEINER
Your paper, not mine. I want no part of it.

DR MORAN
Of course. I was merely trying to further the career of a younger and more attractive colleague. Forgive me for being overly generous.

DR STEINER

Your experiment, lacking appropriate controls, is going to be fraught with error.

DR MORAN

We experiment. We make mistakes. Others correct our mistakes. It's a hobby to keep scientists off the streets at night. This we call progress...or, if we are in bad mood, we might call it carping. Either way, mankind stumbles forward toward extinction. The great thing about today's experiment is that it can never be repeated again! Einstein's brain can be eaten just once, and so no snot-nosed, drivelling graduate student hell-bent on tenure can call anything I say into question. I merely need to you to be a witness to the extroardinary events that have happened today.

DR STEINER

Everything has happened so fast, I am uncertain what I have witnessed.

DR MORAN

Of course not. But are you going to deny that you heard Sam speak German? How do you explain that?

DR STEINER

I can't. But we have to run a lot more tests.

DR MORAN

Tests? Tests are for undergraduates, to separate the sheep from the goats.... And (Indicating the refrigerator) you can see where the sheep end up. For an experiment to succeed, we advanced scientists know that one must start with the conclusion first and then work our way backward. It saves a lot of time. That's how real scientists work. Generals on the battlefield have all the cannon fodder they want to waste upon trial and error, but science is in a constant race against time. Look at me, Dr Steiner. I am an old man. All I have left are a few hours, days, weeks, months, and with the human digestive tract being what it is, who knows how quickly this great moment will slip away from us.

DR STEINER

Us? Why involve me? What do you expect me to do?

DR MORAN

I expect you to corroborate the fact that, after eating Einstein's brain, Sam began to speak a language he had never spoken before. And, we should also note, for the National Endowment for the Arts, that Sam started to play the violin, an instrument for which he had previously displayed no affinity.

DR STEINER

I'm willing to say he spoke a few sentences in German, but the rest is not true.

DR MORAN

It could have been true.

DR STEINER

It could have been true that the sun rises in the west and sets in the east, but that doesn't work out either. Or maybe you wish to fudge that too!

DR MORAN

Perhaps if you viewed the earth from another planet...a possibility that could, with my connections, be arranged. You must help me save this laboratory.... Remember, Dr Steiner, you need my recommendation. Without my good word, you'll be lucky to get a job sewing buttons on lab coats.

DR STEINER

Are you threatening me?

DR MORAN

My dear, the future of this lab is more important than you or me.

DR STEINER

Don't patronize me. I'm not your dear.

DR MORAN

Sorry...But remember, Dr Steiner, science is half curiosity and half country club, and you are not a member yet. Who will listen to a young P h D with no reputation? No one who matters.

(*The laboratory door swings open.* GOLDBERG *enters. He is smoking a pipe.*)

GOLDBERG

I'm back.

DR MORAN

Out, schnitzel-face!

GOLDBERG

(Starting to back out) Don't you want to hear what I have to say?
(Quotes Einstein) "Do all mathematically possible solutions of the
Schroedinger equation, even in the case of a macro-object, occur in
nature under certain conditions?"

DR MORAN

(To GOLDBERG*)* I can't think about it right now. Can't you see that
Dr Steiner and I are engaged in an intellectual debate of the first
magnitude?

DR STEINER

I'll write a letter to every journal in the country, exposing your hoax.

DR MORAN

It's my friends who edit those journals. Besides, don't you realize
that whistle blowers are despised by one and all. You will be merely
regarded throughout the scientific community as a disgruntled,
paranoid lab assistant on the make. You're in love with a scientist
who works for this lab. He does not return your affections.
Everything you say or do will be seen in the murky light of personal
and professional jealousy.

DR STEINER

I can't believe you are talking to me like this. I have always respected
you, looked up to you.... That is why I came to this lab.

DR MORAN

Everyone knows the only reason you come to this lab is because
Albert stores his dead sheep here.

DR STEINER

Not true!... Oh, I know that Albert cares far more for Elise than he
does for me. I know that now.... I can see by the log how many times
he has signed her out. To think I have ruined my life for him.

DR MORAN

Sex first; brain research second. In the history of the human race, it always has been so....

DR STEINER

I came to this lab because I wanted to add to the sum total of human knowledge.

DR MORAN

Of course. I was an idealist once myself. But you have only yourself to think about. I have the whole future of this lab, all the workers, including Goldberg here, whose families depend upon me. The disappearance of Einstein's brain will put us all out of work unless we have significant results to show for it. Thus, we fudge a few equations, copy out a few learned letters, add a few miscellaneous facts to flesh out the report, and voila! A deluge of grants from the National Science Foundation.

GOLDBERG

"I too committed a monumental blunder some time ago (my experiment on the emission of light with positive rays), but we must not take such failures too seriously. Death alone can save us from making blunders."

DR MORAN

Yes. Death alone saves us from blunders. Or at least allows us to cover up blunders. Einstein, you've given me an idea. Kindly go next door and bring back two meat cleavers....

GOLDBERG

Two meat clevers?

DR MORAN

Borrow them from Kinsey's lab. When you go in there, see if Elise is working there. If she is, tell her to get dressed. I wish to see her.

GOLDBERG

Yes, Doctor. Two cleavers... *(He goes out again.)*

DR STEINER

What are you going to do with the meat cleavers?

DR MORAN

Agnes, I've been thinking. I want to help you. I want to make your life better.

DR STEINER

Then let's forget what has happened here today.

DR MORAN

Agnes, in exchange for your loyalty, your absolute loyalty, I am willing to give you something very precious in return.

DR STEINER

What are you talking about?

DR MORAN

Your rival's head on a silver platter.

DR STEINER

My rival's head?

DR MORAN

To continue our...notice I said "our"...research into the effects of eating human brains, we'll cut up Elise's brain and feed it to Sam. Then we...notice I said "we"...shall take careful notes about what changes Sam undergoes.

DR STEINER

Elise's brain?

DR MORAN

Why not? One less sex researcher and the free world can breathe a little easier. And you shall have Dr Kinsey to yourself.... Winter is approaching. Long nights... Happiness is better in practice than in theory. *(Hands her a Polaroid photo)* Perhaps you would like to study these photos of Elise and Dr Kinsey a bit more closely?

DR STEINER

(Looks at the photos) I doubt if we could learn much from cutting up Elise's brain. It's probably just one deep trough of animal cries.

DR MORAN

That's the spirit.... Consider this, Agnes. Elise speaks both Hawaiian and Italian, two languages heavily dependent upon final vowel sound. Also, she is a gourmet cook. And she's astounding in bed....

DR STEINER

How do you know that, doctor?

DR MORAN

(Fanning DR STEINER's jealousy) A lucky guess!... Now, if, after eating Elise's brain, Sam shows the slightest ability to speak Hawaiian and to roast a suckling pig over an open pit, then we'll have more evidence for our hypothesis.... Isn't that what you want? Less Elise and more evidence?

DR STEINER

I'm so confused.

DR MORAN

No. You're lonely. Studying theoretical physics is akin to entering a monastery, taking vows of chastity. Merely concentrate upon having Albert all to yourself.

(Lab door swings open. GOLDBERG enters again. This time he brings in two shining meat cleavers.)

GOLDBERG

Here are the meat cleavers, Doctor.

(DR MORAN takes the cleavers and immediately hands one to DR STEINER.)

DR MORAN

Thank you, Herr Einstein.Tell me. Did you see Elise?

GOLDBERG

Ja...she was standing about naked, trying to feed a white mouse to a boa constrictor.

DR MORAN

Yes, it's a ritual that gets couples ready for marriage.... Sam, go over there and do some push-ups, some calisthenics...work up an appetite. You're going to have some more matzoh soup.

GOLDBERG

Yes, Herr Doctor. *(He goes to a deserted part of the lab and does push-ups.)*

DR MORAN

Well, Agnes, let's get ready. You stand over there, and I'll stand here. When Elise comes through the door aim for the neck. Above all else, don't harm the brain. We're going to have to remove it as soon as Elise hits the floor.

DR STEINER

Do you think Sam, I mean Herr Einstein, will eat another human brain?

DR MORAN

Brains are like potato chips. You can't eat just one.

(The two doctors, gleaming cleavers in hand, take their places on two sides of the swinging door.)

DR MORAN

The main thing is to be brave, be daring, be innovative. Where would the law of gravity be today if Newton didn't stretch the evidence a bit?

DR STEINER

But gravity works.

DR MORAN

Only because it has received a lot of publicity, support from high places.

ELISE'S VOICE

(From outside the door) Dr Steiner, Sam said you wanted to see me?

(DR MORAN raises his finger to his lips, indicating to DR STEINER that she should be silent.)

DR MORAN

Yes, Elise. Come right in. Dr Kinsey wants you to do something with the dead sheep.

ELISE'S VOICE

Did you say dead sheep?

(As the two doctors remain poised for the kill, the lab door slowly swings open.)

DR MORAN

Yes, I did Elise.... Come in, Elise...come in...

(As the cleavers begin their descent, lights out)

CURTAIN

PRECISION
MACHINES

CHARACTERS

JOSEPH CRUICKSHANK
SANDRA

Originally published in *The Capilano Review, #23*

(Scene: An unfurnished apartment in the process of being painted. Upstage center is a double-door walk-in closet. The doors are wide open, revealing wooden and wire coat hangers. There are no clothes.)

(Time: Tomorrow)

*(*JOSEPH CRUICKSHANK *enters. The apartment belongs to* JOSEPH *and his new wife.* JOSEPH *carries two cardboard boxes heaped high with coat hangers, metal and wooden ones, all tangled together.)*

JOSEPH
I found them. I found the coat hangers you were looking for.

SANDRA'S VOICE
(Off) What did you say?

JOSEPH
I said I found the coat hangers you've been looking for.

*(*SANDRA *enters. She carries white paint.)*

SANDRA
I wish you wouldn't mumble all the time. I have a difficult time understanding you.

JOSEPH
(Hanging the coat hangers) I was yelling.

SANDRA
You were mumbling in a yelling fashion.

JOSEPH
You want everybody in the building to know we've got coat hangers? *(He closes the closet doors.)*

SANDRA
They talk about masturbation in the hallways. What's so shameful about coat hangers?

JOSEPH

Just watch. We'll step out for a couple of hours and the kids will come up and steal them from us. I've seen them go in with scrapers and take a whole new paint job away.

SANDRA

Be careful. This is our first fight. It's going to set the tone for all the rest.

JOSEPH

We've only been married three days and you're already planning a lifetime of fights?

SANDRA

I'm not planning anything. I'm being realistic. People who live together have to fight. It's only natural.

JOSEPH

You could have married Rocky Marciano.

SANDRA

It's important to accept things the way they are.

JOSEPH

It's the heart of science.

SANDRA

It's the backbone of marriage.

JOSEPH

Let's close the doors gently. Give them time to adapt to their new surroundings.

(The doors are closed.)

JOSEPH

Perhaps it's too dark for them in there. Do you think they'll need a night light?

SANDRA

Are you ready to paint, O Great King of the Coat Hangers?

JOSEPH

Quite.

SANDRA

Have I ever told you before how much I hate it when you say *quite*?

JOSEPH

I didn't hear you mention it at the marriage ceremony, if that's what you mean.

SANDRA

It's such an English affectation.

JOSEPH

Well, Cruickshank happens to be a good, old-fashioned English name. What kind of an affectation would you prefer I adopt? Persian? Chinese? Laplandish? Outlandish?

(A crash in the closet.)

SANDRA

You've done it again.

JOSEPH

Done what?

SANDRA

Your stomping around has knocked the coat hangers off again.

JOSEPH

Stomping around? I haven't even moved. Or do I stand still stompishly?

(The closet doors are opened. The coat hangers have fallen to the floor in a heap.)

SANDRA

You've upset them again....

JOSEPH

Please don't use the word *upset*. It's morally ambiguous.

SANDRA

If there's one thing I'm not, I'm not morally ambiguous.

JOSEPH

I didn't say *you* were. I said *upset* was. *Upset. Upset. Upset.*

SANDRA

I should listen to you? You don't even put coat hangers on a bar correctly.

JOSEPH

I didn't realize there was a secret skill to it.

SANDRA

(Replacing hangers) There isn't. You just have to be sure that the hook—that's the rounded part here—goes over the pole—that's the wooden part here.

JOSEPH

May I see that grip again?

SANDRA

Certainly.

JOSEPH

(Replacing hangers) Do you use the overlapping grip with all four fingers around the neck? *(Slams one over the bar)* Or do you use a special twist when the neck hits the bar?

SANDRA

There's no need to get angry at me.

JOSEPH

Well I'm not the one who bought these cheap coat hangers.

SANDRA

They're not cheap. Nothing from Bloomingdale's is cheap.

JOSEPH

Then why don't they work?

SANDRA

They do work. They just don't work for very long.

JOSEPH

Something is shaking the bar. That's all.

(They close the door.)

JOSEPH

(Picks up paintbrush) What grip do you recommend for holding this?

(A crash)

JOSEPH

(Pleased) Aha. Now tell me those aren't cheap coat hangers.

SANDRA

Are you playing some kind of a joke on me?

JOSEPH

I'm not playing a joke on you.

(They open the door. The hangers are in a pile.)

SANDRA

Then why are they falling down?

JOSEPH

I imagine they are falling down because of some mysterious force called gravity. They have gravity in closets, too, my dear.

SANDRA

(Replacing the hangers) Is that right?

JOSEPH

Quite... Now, the bar seems straight. The hooks fit tightly around the bar.

SANDRA

What more do you want?

JOSEPH

Unless these coat hangers are spoiled rotten. *(He throws a coat hanger on the floor and steps on it.)* Take that you rotten coat hanger. We give you the best years of our lives, and what do you do? You turn on us.

SANDRA

Was that an earthquake?

JOSEPH
I didn't feel an earthquake. Did you feel an earthquake?

SANDRA
Maybe it was just one of those silent ones...a small tremor that passed right through the closet, and jiggled everything just long enough to make everything fall down.

JOSEPH
There's only one way to find out.

(He enters the closet. His wife joins him. They stand perfectly still, staring straight out at the audience.)

JOSEPH
Feel anything yet?

SANDRA
Do you?

JOSEPH
Not me.

SANDRA
Not me either

JOSEPH
Sounds like a conversation I had in bed once.

SANDRA
(Starts out) You only think of one thing.

JOSEPH
Wait a minute.

SANDRA
You feel a tremor?

JOSEPH
There's a coat hanger in my shirt.

SANDRA
You're supposed to take the coat hanger out of your shirt before you put it on.

JOSEPH
I don't know how it got here.... Help me, will ya?

(SANDRA *removes a coat hanger from beneath* JOSEPH's *shirt*)

SANDRA
I got it.

JOSEPH
Am I wounded?

SANDRA
I don't think it bites. (*She tosses the coat hanger back into the pile.*)

JOSEPH
What are you doing with it?

SANDRA
There's no sense putting them back if all they're going to do is fall down.

JOSEPH
That's true, but it offends my sense of order to hang clothes on the floor.

(SANDRA *screams and jumps.*)

JOSEPH
What's the matter?

SANDRA
It bit me. One of the coat hangers bit me.

JOSEPH
Which one?

SANDRA
What do you mean which one?

JOSEPH

They didn't all bite you, did they? Was it the one you took out of my back?

SANDRA

I took it out of your shirt, not out of your back.

JOSEPH

We're talking about you, not me.

SANDRA

We're talking about coat hangers. Not about either of us... But I did feel something bite me, and we're both rational adults, so that we know it can't be a coat hanger. So what could have bitten me?

JOSEPH

Perhaps your imagination bit you.

SANDRA

My imagination does not bite.

JOSEPH

A true imagination should.

SANDRA

Look at this welt. Is that my imagination?

JOSEPH

It could be a spider.

SANDRA

That's comforting. If you're going to grasp at straws, why not pick a cottonmouth rattlesnake, not just a lowly spider.

JOSEPH

I tell you here and now that it's more comforting to be bit by a snake or a spider than it is to be bitten by a coat hanger. If you had been bitten by a coat hanger, it would upset all known laws of the universe, and the universe, my dear, is a precision machine, just like these coat hangers here are precision instruments. There is no way to improve upon the shape or function of a coat hanger, just as in thousands of years there have been no ways to improve the shape of a barrel. There should be comfort in that. Better to die amid order than to live amid chaos.

SANDRA
You don't sound very sympathetic.

JOSEPH
I'm sorry, but at least now we can breathe easier.

SANDRA
Why can we breathe easier?

JOSEPH
Because there is something in the closet. It knocked all the hangers to the floor and it bit you. Now that the events of the day have been given a rational explanation, we get on with our painting. The human brain is a precision instrument.

SANDRA
But there's nothing in the closet. Nothing so big that it could have knocked all the clothes hangers off.

JOSEPH
Tricky little bugger, isn't he?

SANDRA
We were both standing there and saw nothing.

JOSEPH
The bar that holds the clothes hangers is a precision instrument. Any little thing could have thrown the balance off, especially with the earth moving in eight different directions at the same time. (*He closes the closet door.*)

SANDRA
Did you see anything in there that could have bitten me?

JOSEPH
I didn't bite you. That eliminates one.

SANDRA

You think I bit myself then? You think this redness is
psychosomatic?... Where are you going?

JOSEPH

Whatever is in there is still in there. We've got it trapped in the closet.
I'm going to get something to kill it with.

SANDRA

What about the coat hanger that was in your shirt?

JOSEPH

You think I should kill it with that?

SANDRA

How do you explain the coat hanger getting inside your shirt.

JOSEPH

I don't. But let's be satisfied with two out of three. The most
advanced physicist doesn't know everything there is to know about
the atom. *(He exits.)*

SANDRA

Then you admit something's wrong?... I can't hear what you're
saying. You're mumbling. *(She crosses to the refrigerator.)* I need
something to drink. *(She opens the refrigerator door. Three hundred coat
hangers tumble out.)*

SANDRA

Joseph!

(JOSEPH *returns. He carries a tennis racquet.)*

JOSEPH

(Surveying the scene) What did you let them out for?

SANDRA

I didn't let them out. I opened the refrigerator and there they were.

JOSEPH

What do you mean *there they were*?

SANDRA

I mean they were there...inside the refrigerator.

JOSEPH

Are these the same ones? Or are they different ones?

SANDRA

How would I know? They all look alike to me.

JOSEPH

Now THAT really will upset them.

SANDRA

Did you put them in there?

JOSEPH

Did I put what in where?

SANDRA

Did you put our clothes hangers inside the refrigerator?

JOSEPH

What for?

SANDRA

Joseph, you're annoying me.

JOSEPH

A little precision in language wouldn't hurt right now.

SANDRA

When we were moving, did you put things inside the refrigerator to save space.

JOSEPH

You can't save space. Space is always the same. Except when it's expanding.

SANDRA

You know what I mean.

JOSEPH

I know what you mean, but we didn't move the refrigerator.
This one came with the apartment. Perhaps the previous tenant
put them in there.

SANDRA

Who in God's name would put three hundred coat hangers in a
refrigerator? For what reason? Pourquoi?

JOSEPH

Pourquoi?

SANDRA

Why?

JOSEPH

Some things we have to take on faith. If a human being wishes to
store his or her clothes hangers in a refrigerator, who are we to say
no? Must we impose our will upon someone we haven't even met?

(From the closet there is a crash.)

SANDRA

There it is again.

JOSEPH

We'll get it this time. Take this while I open the doors.
(He hands SANDRA *the tennis racquet.)*

SANDRA

What's this for?

JOSEPH

When I open the door, whatever comes out, hit it. Hit it good and
hard.

SANDRA

Is this all you could find?

JOSEPH

No. I also found our color television set but, I didn't think it would
be very practical right now.

SANDRA
Why should there be a crash in the closet? There was nothing in there to fall down.

JOSEPH
Maybe the pole fell down.

(He opens the doors. There on the pole are all the coat hangers, swaying gently. Three or four hang down, interlocked together.)

JOSEPH
Now that's impossible.

SANDRA
Thank God!

JOSEPH
What are you thanking God for?

SANDRA
Because now we know that the hangers in there are not the same as the hangers out here.

JOSEPH
(Looking inside the closet) Systems of philosophy have been built upon less.

SANDRA
There's nothing in the closet. Right?

JOSEPH
They're linked together. Can't you see that some of these hangers are linked together?

SANDRA
There is nothing in the closet.

JOSEPH
I can't pull them apart.

SANDRA
Not even anything small.

JOSEPH

Solid cannot pass through solid.

SANDRA

But something did bite me.

JOSEPH

It's a precise law of physics.

SANDRA

And coat hangers don't fall down by themselves.

JOSEPH

The closet's built against a solid brick wall.

SANDRA

Nobody I know keeps clothes hangers in the refrigerator.

JOSEPH

A few moments ago I was perfectly content.

SANDRA

You open a refrigerator and they come spilling out.

JOSEPH

Je suis content.

SANDRA

What can be worse than a cold clothes hanger?

JOSEPH

It is impossible for a happy man to live in a universe where objects fall upward and people fall out.

SANDRA

I should call Mama and tell her not to send the trunks.

JOSEPH

Where shall we hide if coat hangers revert to laws of the jungle?

SANDRA

Let's have another conversation like this sometime.

JOSEPH

Form follows function.

SANDRA

Call it counterpoint. You take the A line.

JOSEPH

What did people do before they had coat hangers to comfort them?

SANDRA

I'll take the B line.

JOSEPH

Was there comfort in a world without coat hangers?

SANDRA

You say one thing and I'll say another thing.

JOSEPH

I went out of the room.

SANDRA

See if we meet.

JOSEPH

Not if I go out of the room, and if you stay here.

SANDRA

What would Harold Pinter say in a situation like this?

JOSEPH

I stepped out. You opened the closet and hung up the hangers.

SANDRA

Precisely.

JOSEPH

And then you welded three coat hangers together, linking them forever so that not the greatest brute force could wrench them apart.

SANDRA

All in less than a minute.

JOSEPH

Oh no. You planned all this out ahead of time. Putting three hundred coat hangers inside the refrigerator. Just waiting for an opening, a chance to mock the world of reason. There is a secret passageway. Where?

SANDRA

I am supposing. Suppose there is a secret passageway. You leave the room, enter the closet secretly, hang up the hangers while I'm distracted by the pile of hangers spilling out of the refrigerator which you had put there ahead of time. It was you that introduced the interlocking hangers.

JOSEPH

I am an anthropologist not a practical joker.

SANDRA

An anthropologist in public. In the closet a practical joker.

JOSEPH

I have no motive. You lack a motive.

SANDRA

To drive me insane which you have succeeded doing beyond your wildest expectations.

JOSEPH

I have nothing to gain by driving you insane. For God's sake, I've just married you.

SANDRA

You an educated man! Since when are marriage and insanity mutually contradictory?

JOSEPH

Bosh!

SANDRA

Quite.... Not satisfied with my body you must get your fingers on my mind as well.

JOSEPH

It's you who's doing this to me. After all, you stand to collect insurance money.

SANDRA

Your college is so generous. What should I do with all that money?

JOSEPH

Buy yourself some clothes to go with all these hangers of yours!

SANDRA

They're not mine. They're ours. This is community property.

JOSEPH

We're getting upset.

SANDRA

That word isn't precise!

JOSEPH

We should be uniting together.

SANDRA

I don't see how we can unite apart.

JOSEPH

We must face this problem squarely like mature adults.

SANDRA

There is nothing to be afraid of.

JOSEPH

We are together, not attacking each other. Neither of us wants to harm the other.

SANDRA

Violence is the heart of sex.

JOSEPH

Not for us. Stiff upper lip.

SANDRA

I'm not playing a joke on you. Are you playing a joke on me?

JOSEPH

No.

SANDRA

Where does that leave us?

JOSEPH

Damn!

SANDRA

What?

JOSEPH

Another one has crawled under my shirt again. *(He removes a coat hanger from beneath his shirt.)*

SANDRA

Is it the same one?

JOSEPH

Can it possibly make any difference at all?

SANDRA

You asked me if they were the same.

JOSEPH

Things are different with you.

SANDRA

Maybe there is one coat hanger out of all these that has a great need for body warmth.

JOSEPH

Sandy, I'm going back in there.

SANDRA

No, Joseph, don't.

JOSEPH

I have to. Everything I believe about the world is at stake.

SANDRA

Go to darkest Africa instead. Another anthropological mission.

JOSEPH

But why?

SANDRA

Because in Africa they have trained guides. There's no guide for this closet.

JOSEPH

There's nothing to worry about.

SANDRA

How can you say that?

JOSEPH

I'll take this flashlight. I'll take the tennis racquet. If you hear me knock on the door open it immediately. That's all there is to it.

SANDRA

I don't want to be a widow on my honeymoon.

JOSEPH

You're overreacting.

SANDRA

I'm not overreacting. I'm underreacting.

(JOSEPH enters the closet and shuts the door.)

SANDRA

Is anything happening?

JOSEPH

I just got inside.

SANDRA

It's not a good idea. The air's not good.

JOSEPH

I have plenty of air.

(A pause. Then JOSEPH knocks on the door. SANDRA pulls the door open.)

SANDRA

Joseph! You all right?

(JOSEPH *emerges with a coat hanger around his neck.*)

SANDRA

What happened?

JOSEPH

Nothing happened. There are just no batteries in this flashlight.

SANDRA

You should have checked it before you went inside. You're losing all semblance of professional training.

JOSEPH

It's your flashlight!

SANDRA

When did I become the supply sergeant all of a sudden?

JOSEPH

I'll use my lighter.

SANDRA

You'll start a fire.

JOSEPH

There's nothing to set fire to. There's nothing in the closet but metal coat hangers.

SANDRA

What happened to them all?

JOSEPH

What do you mean what happened to them all?

SANDRA

They're all gone.... Most of them are gone.

JOSEPH

Perhaps they sensed a hostile atmosphere.

SANDRA

Why don't you say something about the coat hanger around your neck?

JOSEPH

Why don't you say something about it? You're the one who's good at instigating conversations.

SANDRA

Quite.

JOSEPH

Every inanimate object in the world is making fun of me. Must you too?

SANDRA

Coat hangers are not every inanimate object.

JOSEPH

When I count to ten I want all those coat hangers back where they belong. And then we'll consider the whole subject closed.

SANDRA

Don't threaten me. I have nothing to do with it.

JOSEPH

No?

SANDRA

No.

JOSEPH

Whose idea was it to hang up our clothes in the first place? I'd just as soon keep my clothes dangling over chairs. A chair you can trust. A chair doesn't crawl up under your shirt.

SANDRA

Get it through your pedantic skull. I have nothing to do with anything that is happening, any time, any place.

JOSEPH

Things don't just happen by themselves.

SANDRA

Then let's admit it to each other. This place is haunted. There's such a thing as a haunted house.

JOSEPH

You call that a rational explanation?

SANDRA

Why not? Ghosts are precision machines like anything else.

JOSEPH

Oiled only by primitive superstition. We have risen far above the apes, the animals, the savage.

SANDRA

There isn't an ape in the Bronx Zoo plagued by a coat hanger problem.

JOSEPH

(Counting) One...two...three...four...five.

SANDRA

There. Are you happy now?

(A solitary coat hanger slides slowly along the rod and stops on and in the center of the rod.)

JOSEPH

I am happy in a world where five comes after four, not after three, not after two, but after four.

SANDRA

It slid back all by itself.

(A second coat hanger slides along the pole and joins the first one.)

SANDRA

We didn't offer it any food or anything.

JOSEPH

I'm going right back in there. We'll try it again.

SANDRA

No, Joseph. Please! We must let well enough alone.

JOSEPH

When you hear me hit my fist against the door, open it immediately. If there's a ghost in that closet, I'm going to find out about it by God.

SANDRA
Then you agree with me that ghosts are causing this to happen.

JOSEPH
No. I don't agree with you. The Greeks never had ghosts in their civilization! That's what made them so much more human.
(*He enters the closet and shuts the door. There is a long pause.*)

SANDRA
Joseph? Are you all right?

(*A coat hanger slides out from beneath the closet door. Then a second one.*)

SANDRA
Joseph. Are you sliding coat hangers from beneath the door?

JOSEPH
What are you talking about?

(*A third coat hanger slides out from beneath the door.*)

SANDRA
There's another one.... You're just doing that to scare me.

JOSEPH
I'm not doing anything to scare anybody.

SANDRA
They're all getting out.

JOSEPH
(*Still in closet*)They can't. I have the exit blocked.

SANDRA
(*Pushes them back*) I'm sending them back.

JOSEPH
I don't want them.

SANDRA
Can you see anything?

JOSEPH
I've got my lighter on. I can see everything.

(The doorbell rings.)

SANDRA

What do you see?

(The doorbell rings.)

JOSEPH

Nothing.

SANDRA

(Calling to door) I'm busy now.

(She pushes coat hangers back. More slide out. The doorbell continues ringing.)

SANDRA

All right. All right.

JOSEPH

Who are you talking to?

SANDRA

I'll be right back. Don't go away.

(SANDRA exits. The coat hangers still slide out from beneath the closet door.)

JOSEPH

Sandra!

(JOSEPH pounds on the closet door. Each pounding is slightly more desperate than the one before it. There is a pause.)

(SANDRA returns with a cardboard box. She opens it. Inside are the coat-hangers she had ordered from Bloomingdale's.)

SANDRA

Joseph! Here are the coat hangers we ordered from Bloomingdales.

(No response)

SANDRA

Joseph, are you all right in there?

(No response)

SANDRA
Are you still in there?... Joseph, answer me!

(SANDRA *opens the closet door. There, inside, is* JOSEPH *hanging in a noose fashioned of coat hangers. His tongue protrudes. His eyes bulge. He is clearly dead.*)

(SANDRA *screams.*)

SANDRA
Oh, my darling...Joseph...Joseph...speak to me....

(*She enters the closet in an attempt to release her husband from the grip of the coat hangers. She strikes out wildly against the coat hangers that have returned to their places on the rod.*)

SANDRA
Killers!... Murderers!... That's all you are.... You're precision killers....

(*Her arms and legs are entangled in the piles of hangers that have fallen [leapt?] to the floor. The closet door slowly shuts upon her. We hear the crash of coat hangers.*)

SANDRA'S VOICE
Stop it ! Let go of me!... Get your filthy hooks off me...

(*Silence*)

(*The doorbell rings.*)

(*A solitary coat hanger slides out beneath the door.*)

VOICE FROM OFF-STAGE
Hello in there!... I'm your neighbor from across the hall. Did you people by any chance leave some coat hangers in the hallway?

(*As if by way of an answer, the coat hanger begins its journey toward the front door.*)

(*Lights out*)

CURTAIN